MORE

A Tur[

RAY WADDLE has held up this buzzing, booming collection of spiritual treasure as a distant mirror; focusing its light and truth into the nooks and corners of our frenzied and troubled lives. The psalmists monitor our mind and soul with the piercing thoroughness of a spiritual MRI. Mr. Waddle has superbly interpolated between those voices and moods and ours. Most of all, he commends these ancient lodestones to us by conveying his deep love for them.

—Kenneth Briggs
Author, lecturer, and former *New York Times* religion writer

COMBINING A reporter's inclination to dig up facts with a genuine fondness for familiar material, Ray Waddle has produced a commentary on the Psalms that has the immediacy of a news story and the beauty of age-old truths, with a special twenty-first century relevance.

—Jane Hines
Editor, *Presbyterian Voice*

A TURBULENT Peace

THE PSALMS FOR OUR TIME

Ray Waddle

UPPER ROOM BOOKS®
NASHVILLE

A TURBULENT PEACE
The Psalms for Our Time
Copyright © 2003 by Ray Waddle
All rights reserved.

The Upper Room® Web site: www.upperroom.org

Scriptures designated KJV are taken from The King James Version of the Bible.

Cover and interior design: Ellisor Design
First printing: 2003

ISBN: 0-8358-9873-3

Printed in the United States of America

To
Lisa

CONTENTS

ACKNOWLEDGMENTS

The Psalms are full of gratitude and complaint. Here I offer only gratitude. Thanks go to Dan Beck, Rick Christensen, Tom Nuccio, and John Reiman for taking a hard look at the manuscript.

Thanks also to Don Beisswenger, April Benavides, Garlinda Burton, Joe Calloway, Will Campbell, Christ Church Cathedral, Jeff Clark, Virgil Harry, Amy Hooper, Ken Kanter, Palmer and Beverly Mai, J. J. Rosen, Benjamin and Virginia Tate, Vanderbilt Divinity School, Paul and Helen Waddle, and Alan Waddle.

Thanks as well to Frank Sutherland and *The Tennessean* newsroom for letting a reporter find his way on the religion beat year after year, the best assignment in daily journalism.

And thanks to my wife, Lisa, who shows me every day what's possible.

INTRODUCTION
God's Secret Place of Thunder

As a deer longs for flowing streams, so my soul longs for you,
O God. (Psalm 42:1)

Yet you are near, O LORD,
and all your commandments are true. (Psalm 119: 151)

He it is who makes the clouds rise at the end of the earth;
he makes lightnings for the rain
and brings out the wind from his storehouses. (Psalm 135:7)

You desire truth in the inward being;
therefore teach me wisdom in my secret heart. (Psalm 51:6)

S ometimes you see one on the highway, a little sign nailed to a tree with a single-word message stenciled in red: *Repent.* The sign is always anonymous. No attribution. To the passing driver, it might be the latest odd bit of road art or an anxious gesture of countryside piety—or something else. Flashing past you at sixty miles per hour, the *Repent* sign might trigger an unexpected emotion, a spear of feeling rising from childhood or from the memory bank of civilization itself, a stubborn theme from the human story persisting for four thousand years.

The sheer volume of tasks to do every day, the stuff to buy, and e-mails to answer tends to drown out the old wonder and wisdom. We dismiss the ancient stories and books as too slow to deliver the daily advantage in the neon global economy. The digitized, overscheduled life crowds out the space for thinking, the space for hearing one's own questions and answers.

Yet the desperately new never totally replaces the old; they mingle. Despite the corrosive haste and hustle of twenty-four-hour consumerism, an ancient benchmark survives for measuring the days and enduring the nights. It shimmers in the background of distracted routine. It's not discussed much in public life or in the boardrooms of power and celebrity, but it's there—a glowing ore, debated, embraced, rejected, clarified, denied, intimated, and dis-covered every day: the Bible.

The Bible. The words provoke reaction—sweet feelings or resentment, nostalgia or boredom, or a mood more complicated and fierce. Open the

Bible and a strange world of sacred wind and mighty acts comes pouring out. Its stormy contents mingle with another strange world, ours, the civilization of asphalt, movies, computers, wildflowers, honky-tonks, and terrorism. This is where people read the Bible—at the intersection of ancient religion and contemporary daily life. The goings-on of Noah, Jeremiah, Sarah, and Jesus of Nazareth jostle against the morning's thoughts of doing paperwork, field work, yard work, homework.

Despite the ideology of the ever-new, America in its millennial-minded soul still regards the Bible as the holy book. Gallup polls consistently report that more than half of the American people read the Bible at least occasionally. People still fight over it. The religion news headlines of recent decades have been dominated by "battles for the Bible," power struggles between liberals and conservatives who use scripture to endorse their own slate of social values and condemn their opponents'. Unaffected by these noisy debates, the Bible remains the personal playbook of eternity for millions; the repository of sacred stories, touchstones, and phrases that gives symbolic solemnity to public occasions and private longings—even for people who never actually read it. Maybe especially for them: The power of symbols runs deepest when it goes undetected, unexamined.

Some people just plain stay away from it. The Bible feels too alien from their everyday psychological life. Maybe they're still bruised from childhood Sunday school memories of clumsy adults who failed to make religion relevant. An instinct of self-preservation stops them from giving it a glance. To read it is to risk changing one's relationship to it. The Bible might be a more surprising document—intriguing, jarring, life-changing—than they thought.

For those inclined to crack the Bible's shell, their encounter with its long-ago personalities, delivered curbside in the here-and-now, carries with it unspoken cargo, a mysterious communiqué addressed personally to each reader. It bears the same sort of news that wafts up from old hymns or the silence of the High Plains or the serenity of a country church—the so-big-you-miss-it story of human life; a chronicle of birth, death, breakthrough, evil, redemption, tears, delight, awe. The Bible's contents survived transport across thousands of years, against all odds of weather, political violence, and poor translations. The Bible's very endurance is a kind of miracle. For its readers, no matter the faith affiliation, the Bible contains news that addresses the secret narrative of their lives: Their personal story connects with a larger spiritual drama playing out in shadows behind it all.

Life these days feels faster and scarier; it's hard to catch up with ourselves, hard to edit and delete the mounting heaps of clutter and insecurity. All the while, the Bible sits on the shelf, waiting in a place of stillness, unchanged, unblinking, inviting scrutiny. Full of perplexity and intrigue, it steadies readers who swear by it. Serenely patient, the Bible is unbamboozled by the passing glamour or hysteria of the moment. It seems to have a mind of its own.

❧

Somewhere near the middle of this thick book called scripture, protected by the hardback cover and the layers of entries on either side (Genesis at one end, Revelation at the other if it's the Christian Bible), resides the book of Psalms. The Psalms, all 150 of them, lie nestled there like the Bible's own beating heart. We know surprisingly little about how they came to be. They're part of the Hebrew Bible, or Old Testament, and were written in Hebrew as expressions of the Jewish faith. An honored tradition affirms that most were written by King David himself (ca. 1010–970 B.C.E.), the musician-king who shaped the early personality of ancient Israel. Many scholars today discount the broad claim that David composed many of them, saying instead that anonymous poets or Temple singers after David's time (probably between 800–200 B.C.E.) wrote most of them. Psalms were composed as hymns, prayers, or liturgies for use in the holy temple in Jerusalem at the time. Some psalms became so popular that families probably recited them at home, outside the official precincts of organized religion. No one knows all the details of their use. Many psalms include notations like "selah." No one is sure what they mean. ("Selah" possibly indicates a rest or interlude between verses.)

Scholars believe the Psalms were set to music, but there's no consensus about what the music sounded like. Meager evidence survives. So only half the spirit of the Psalms is available to us: the words but not the music. There's a harsh symbolism in that. It's how we often read the Bible now—in one dimension only, a landscape without sound.

Still, the Psalms have always managed to communicate to Jews, Christians, and other readers. They are a birthright of every believer, gems from the biblical treasury. In this part of scripture, believers have the floor to speak to their hearts' content: The Psalms are human yearnings addressed to the Almighty, often followed by the Almighty's response. Their popularity resides in their remarkable emotional range and motley voices, sometimes as a congregation of believers, sometimes as an individual in turmoil or reverie. It's a jolt to realize how moody the Psalms are. Full of praise of God, they also hanker, plead, and pester God for forgiveness or mercy. There are dramatic emotional ups and downs, uncensored feelings of anger toward other people, toward enemies, toward God or the absence of God. The turbulence of the Psalms is one of their best-kept secrets. That turbulence, that ill-mannered lack of decorum, does not get much play in the sanctuaries and brochures of official faith.

If the Psalms had been neglected, the climate changed after the terrorist attacks of 9/11. In a million places of prayer after the slaughter, Americans rediscovered the Psalms. At nearly every gathering of grief, the roll call—Psalm 23; Psalm 46; Psalm 121; Psalm 145—was heard, read, or sung in unison, pouring into countless broken hearts.

People discovered a place to channel their own rage, exhaustion, and need for solace: "The LORD is near to the brokenhearted." "God is our refuge and strength, a very present help in trouble." "In your presence there is fullness of joy." "Even though I walk through the darkest valley, I fear no evil." They found their own emotions embedded and ennobled in the words of these sacred psalms, nearly a thousand years in the making, the cumulative passion of a biblical people calling out to God in grief and gratitude. The words had not been felt so deeply in America, at least not since World War II or perhaps even the Civil War. Emotions very ancient were stirred and revisited.

⁂

This book began as a sleepless series of scribbles in a notebook at three AM. My aim at such an ungodly hour was to trace some restless, nagging thoughts about my day job.

For nearly twenty years I was the religion writer for the morning newspaper in one of the biggest religion hubs in America, Nashville. I started reading the Psalms in order to make sense of what I saw every day—new announcements of divine revelation, spiritual quests, inspirational life stories, dignified struggles of faith, mutant theologies, colossal businesses built to do the work of the Lord, good deeds and suspicious claims, all in the name of God and scripture. Every day I monitored the traffic sounds of the religious life—the collisions, screeches, and revving engines at the corner of biblical faith and modern life.

In the still mostly Protestant South and in worship-going America, the Bible remains the iron lung of the sacred life, the oxygen tank, primary text, owner's manual, and distinct revelation from God. Some people know its words and live by them quietly day after day. Others promote the Bible without knowing what it actually says. Gallup polls say the Psalms are the most beloved of the books of scripture. Surely the Psalms hold a clue, I thought, to these ever-renewing passions of faith inside America. In the small hours of the night, I decided to take a harder look.

Read the Psalms one after another; sit long enough with their echoes, and all sorts of notions and commotions, ideas and peeves begin bouncing off the page. My adventure through the Psalms was a journey of making sense of them—what the psalm authors meant, what the Psalms mean now, how they add to or subtract from one's assumed belief about the Almighty, how they correct one's thoughts about the nature of faith and affirm or contradict the partisan arguments about the will of God in our time.

I took each psalm in succession and wrote what came to mind. The effort became a kind of psalms memoir—not an academic exercise or a preachy epistle (usually) but a weave of thoughts about the ancient words on the page, along with anecdotes from the many expressions of public faith and spiritual trends I'd witnessed, as well as my own occasional outbursts of conviction. I read the King James Version to see what treasures could still be wrung from that four-hundred-year-old translation. But I relied finally on a modern translation—the New Revised Standard Version—because it usually succeeds better than the King James at communicating the sense of each psalm in today's terms. I divided this study into five sections, following the traditional (though rather mysterious) division of the Psalms into five parts or "books."

Some of the encounters that follow are meditations based on a mere phrase or two from a psalm, a verse or word that wells up through the cracks, suddenly flooding the emotional sky with sound and light. The Psalms work that way on a reader. Deprived of their original music, they wait there, monumentally, for the next reader, the next encounter, regardless of setting or century. The words generate a music of their own, coming, as Psalm 81 puts it, from a "secret place of thunder."

❧

This is not a scholarly analysis of each psalm. With care and wisdom, scholars every day address various technical questions about the Psalms—the way they were put together, the different types of psalms, the internal theologies and issues of when or why they were written. I'm a writer but no Bible technician, no preacher or Hebrew language expert. My approach is to take each psalm as it appears in English, raw and unvarnished, the way most people take it, and see how it exposes itself to the air that surrounds a reader today. I consulted a couple of thick commentaries regularly along the way, notably the *Harper's Bible Commentary* and *The Interpreter's One-Volume Commentary on the Bible*, as well as the *Oxford Companion to the Bible* and *The New Oxford Annotated Bible* (NRSV). Other useful studies include *Out of the Depths: The Psalms Speak for Us Today* by Bernhard W. Anderson with Steven Bishop and *The Psalms: An Introduction* by James L. Crenshaw.

Nevertheless, this book essentially records the journey of one reader paddling on a sea of words with no cell phone, no clergy certification, just a few books and a boatload of impressions, outrage, and wonder to fuel the getting there. No doubt it's a Protestant compulsion—a lone reader hunched over the text, seeking minimal intrusion from the authorities. The widely proclaimed authority of the Holy Bible means nothing unless an individual can set out to mark its risings and movements from where he or she is. We each face our own soul's reckoning and homecoming, and we each read by our own lights, as individuals all suited up and ready to stay in the game until the final tick.

The book of Psalms is not the country I thought I knew. There are cries of agony, wisdom, obscurities, breakthroughs of poetry, news that doesn't make the daily headlines. What follows is a record of the news I found there.

BOOK I

A LITTLE LOWER
than *God*

PSALM 1: *Newsworthy*

Happy are those
> *who do not follow the advice of the wicked, . . .*
> *or sit in the seat of scoffers.*

M ost days I sit at my desk, buffeted by phone calls, e-mails, and snow-drifts of mail from denominational offices, and try to write religion stories. I should be returning the phone call of a local guy who has an urgent message from God for the world. He'll have to wait a bit. The pressure of other stories intervenes—a Unitarian-Universalist convention, a pentecostal preach-fest, a new book on the interventions of angels in the lives of Americans. Next week, there's a profile to do on a Christian comedian, the anniversary of a Hindu temple, a symposium on the saintly Dr. Albert Schweitzer.

The religion scene can be a taxing paradox. After a while, it's easy to sink into "the seat of scoffers," to use Psalm 1's unexpected phrase, and be weary of it all. The claims of each faith jostle one another and rub themselves raw. Each raises a flag for God, using the language of battle to define spiritual winners and losers. Believers tell their stories with courage and grace, or with anxious shouting under battle conditions, hoping to establish a beachhead in the public realm and spiritual marketplace. They do so without embarrassment about the scads of competing claims that are just as passionate as theirs. Such is the endless stream of faith in America. All seek high ground, ultimate truth, a sky's mansion, a citadel for holding back the inhuman forces.

Sometimes if I sit still, an awareness comes like a breeze, an awareness of the Bible's curious power to speak to each reader: "Their delight is in the law of the LORD. . . . They are like trees planted by streams of water, which yield their fruit in its season." In a few short lines, Psalm 1 launches such a quest.

And I sit there, still as a tree, despite the stress of an ordinary Tuesday, and think from a place where the smoke has cleared and creativity and refreshment stir. I wonder if this is how God beckons, breathing an opening into the middle of an office day. The vista looks inward, even as the public collisions of belief in America reach furious, outrageous, newsworthy levels.

And on his law they meditate day and night.

PSALM 2: *Laughter and Anger Divine*

He who sits in the heavens laughs.

Heavenly laughter, decrees from kings, coronation speeches—to twenty-first-century ears, such notions might seem far away, like a noble stage production from another time, Shakespearean almost. Psalm 2 is uttered by a king of Israel, perhaps at his own coronation. The political details are no longer known. He speaks as one of God's anointed; he vents against heathen, hostile rival rulers who plot rebellion. It's in vain, he declares. God's in control. In heaven God laughs the last laugh.

Every day the stage of mind and heart opens on the possibility of God—sometimes remote, other times vivid and hot to the touch. Some people envision God as the deity on the throne who keeps a lordly eye on the big picture. Others regard God as the busy stage manager of our affairs. Yet others feel the burdensome absence of God from the stage itself: The stage is empty and unlit, though furnished with props for a future performance if we would only schedule time to attend.

Frequently we keep these musings about God to ourselves, the secret hunches that visit our days and nights. It's not always easy to find a safe place to hash them out. Conversations about God become a hushed exercise, hesitant, embarrassed.

In this era, most people perhaps save their bigger-than-life emotions for ceremonies outside the congregational walls—arena rock concerts, stock car races, dinner out. It's fun to partake of the rising sound of a Saturday night out, especially with friends, especially in a self-aware restaurant. Every city of a certain size has such a café, and everybody in the place knows the feeling if it's that kind of night. Thoughts of ancient anointed kings are distant indeed. After a hard week at work, we try to anoint ourselves with the myth-enhancing qualities of wine or swaggering opinion or keen-eyed observance of strangers across the way.

Meanwhile, the theater of the Psalms—God's blessing, God's turbulence—plays on, awaiting our notice.

> *Serve the LORD with fear, with trembling kiss his feet,*
> *or he will be angry, and you will perish in the way;*
>   *for his wrath is quickly kindled.*
>
> *Happy are all who take refuge in him.*

PSALM 3: *Enchanted*

I lie down and sleep;
I wake again, for the LORD sustains me.

No one admits it, but one of the last enchantments we allow ourselves now is dream life. Enchantment in the old-fashioned sense of magical charm comes only in sleep. In dreams, things bizarrely appear and disappear without explanation or obvious beginning or end, without logic or apology.

By day we test every experience on the anvil of logic. Busy people furtively hold out hope for the possibility of religious ecstasy, the ego's reckless merger with something bigger and transcendent. But for the record, we keep our cool.

Logic keeps its hold on religious style too, on the enchantments of faith. Arguments about religion logically rack up an impressive catalog of enemies. By sheer power of rational thought, we can deduce and locate every enemy of faith and put a label on everybody. We'll stand against liberals or conservatives, Muslims or Mormons or Moravians, because they don't conform to precise word-for-word formulations of familiar religious doctrine. Enemies multiply according to every possible combination of wrong answers to the question: "Do you know the road to salvation?"

By bedtime we reluctantly concede a short respite from the wars of belief and certitude and turn to sleep. In Psalm 3, sleep means a temporary break from the litany of enemies and slights, real and imagined: "O LORD, how many are my foes! Many are rising against me. . . . But you, O LORD, are a shield around me, my glory, and the one who lifts up my head."

Sleep is the place of untroubled breath and healing. In Psalm 3, sleep provides a zone of God's protection. Trolling the nighttime landscape of dreams, anything is possible, including encounters with divine messengers who by the light of day we'd scoff at and send away for all kinds of logical reasons.

I cry aloud to the LORD,
and he answers me from his holy hill.

PSALM 4: *King David*

But know that the LORD has set apart the faithful for himself;
the LORD hears when I call to him.

P salm 4, like nearly half the psalms in the whole book, includes a nota-
tion at the top saying "A Psalm of David." Hence the traditional belief
that David wrote the Psalms. Even rock stars assume so. U2's Bono calls
David the Elvis of the Bible—a celebrity of biblical proportion, cultural
icon, pivotal personality of charm and catastrophe.

David is indeed one of the extraordinary figures of world history. The
Bible presents him warts and all in the book of Second Samuel and elsewhere—a gifted leader and musician close to God's heart, an anguished
political dynamo who also committed adultery and had the woman's husband put in harm's way and killed. With such a big personality bestriding the
Hebrew Bible, it's easy to read the Psalms with David's voice in mind, for the
Psalms are full of pleas to God, like those of a man intimate with the faith of
ancient Israel: "The LORD hears when I call to him."

Scholars doubt that David wrote most of the psalms as they now appear.
More likely, later artists and devotees did the composing, people of the royal
Israelite court of David's lineage, long after David died around 970 B.C.E. The
tradition that David wrote the Psalms formed centuries after they came to
be, according to this argument.

It doesn't much matter. The character of David, whatever he wrote or
didn't write, is a gift to every reader. Scripture preserves him in all his flawed
complexity. His life was often R-rated, not ready for prime-time family
viewing. Maybe it's inaccurate to say he wrote this psalm or that. But it
amazes many a reader to know that such a towering, stumbling figure as
David walked into the pages of holy scripture. A man of errors and of faith,
he audaciously called on God. Reading the Psalms, taking up their spirit of
divine access even now, implies a similar audacity.

I will both lie down and sleep in peace;
for you alone, O LORD, make me lie down in safety.

PSALM 5: *Down to Business*

Give ear to my words, O LORD.

The religion business in America is an impressive maelstrom of publishing, piety, and profit. My Protestant preacher friend had another view: "It's just a lot of holy talk."

What bothered him was the loose God-talk that fills the air, a smear of patter that doesn't know where real spirituality ends and self-serving commercialism begins.

In Nashville, a premier center for Christian publishing and music, religious talk is a way of life, a vocational calling, the currency of daily business. The Lord's work is a billion-dollar deal built on the details of rail distribution, copy deadlines, music celebrity, bottom-line efficiencies, takeovers, promotions, and prayer before meetings. Through it all, the Holy Bible is a daily touchstone.

The holy commerce flourishes at street level too. Guitar strummers and unpublished authors seek to land a contract for their late-night revelations. Religious trends arrive claiming the end is near. Day after tomorrow, they're gone. A crowded kingdom of words and publicity spin gold and fool's gold. Career ambitions and longings for God mingle in the air.

Sometimes bad feeling gets churned up by so much official faith. Bitter ex-employees of a Christian business come forward to say they've been fired in an ungodly fashion. Or spiritual refugees float by, disillusioned by a rigid pastor and now seeking a larger truth on which to lay their head.

"It's just a lot of holy talk," the minister sighed. He'd been wounded by church politics and in-fighting in his time. His career as distinguished pastor and author was coming to a tattered end. The opposition party had taken over the denomination's boardrooms and bank accounts, disdaining his political agenda and leaving him isolated.

Psalm 5 is a cry against enemies and empty flatterers, a pledge to be faithful. Every morning, the glassy denominational offices in town open their doors again and get down to business, renewing the wager that this is not just cheap talk but the real thing.

O LORD, in the morning you hear my voice;
in the morning I plead my case to you, and watch.

PSALM 6: *Old-Fashioned Dread*

I am weary with my moaning; . . .
I drench my couch with my weeping.

Metaphysical dread—it's a phrase you don't hear much now. It went out of fashion years ago, along with beret-capped existentialism, Bergman movies, and other conspicuous displays of thoughtful exertion. Metaphysical dread, fear of the eternal void, nothingness—they sound overblown, attention-getting, too cerebral for a climate of Seinfeld reruns and Nasdaq box scores and other daily entertainments that serve to numb the deep anxieties.

Yet the writer of Psalm 6 sweats and shakes with dread and terror, the metaphysical variety, writing in a very personal manner. The psalm writer fears God's abandonment; death is dreadful indeed: "For in death there is no remembrance of you." He seeks no recourse in guardian angels or reassuring sermons.

Standard interpreters say the psalmist is wrestling with physical illness, but surely that's not the whole story. Psalm 6 talks of soul-sickness, not just the physical sort: "O LORD, heal me, for my bones are shaking with terror. My soul also is struck with terror, while you, O LORD—how long?"

It's a fierce business to fend off the free-falling loneliness and fear inside the empty spaces of the universe. It's hard to laugh it off with irony or jokiness. A cry from a place of terrified dread, according to Psalm 6, demands nothing less than a rescue by God, a shattering intimacy with the divine name that can be a terrifying prospect itself, whether you call it metaphysical or not.

Depart from me, all you workers of evil,
for the LORD has heard the sound of my weeping.

PSALM 7: *Guts*

Let the assembly of the peoples be gathered around you,
and over it take your seat on high.

A local group of Bible readers, mostly Christians, recently finished a public experiment to promote the Good Book. As an act of faithfulness they read the whole Bible aloud in public, nonstop.

It took five days and four nights, reading at all hours from a podium in a city park. The group welcomed volunteers and took turns. It was done primarily in English, but local immigrants provided readings in Korean, Spanish, and a half dozen other tongues. Organizers invited the public to come, to sit and listen. Sometimes people came. Sometimes the readers had no audience at all. Scoffers called it a pointless stunt. The readers carried on no matter what, page after page in an unbroken streak from Genesis to Revelation, even at four AM with no one else around, only the glowing streetlights of the sleeping city. The readers knew their job—to send a cascade of words from scripture into the world, like seeds that might take root somewhere, somehow.

In Psalm 7, the writer gives voice to strong personal convictions of faith with a slew of enemies at his heels. In America it doesn't cost much to read the Bible or believe its contents. No persecutor's midnight knock on the door will interrupt the prayer group. Faith is not a life-and-death political ordeal as it is in some countries. In the land of freedom, it's harder to test belief. So people undertake feats of spiritual strength to challenge their stamina. They drag a cross across the length of the nation or memorize an entire sacred text. The Bible marathon folks were pushing themselves too, seeking enough people to read Holy Writ out loud all night, in public, all the begats and everything else. And they did it.

Verse 9 says God tests people's hearts and minds. The King James Version says "hearts and reins." *Reins* is an old word for kidneys, the traditional seat of the emotions. When you agree to get up at three AM to read scripture outdoors, it's surely your gut, the heart and reins, and the echo chamber of the divine that's talking to you, despite the skeptics, despite the silent night sky.

Judge me, O LORD, according to . . . the integrity that is in me.

Psalm 8: *Glory*

Yet you have made them a little lower than God.

Psalm 8 serves up a monumental mission statement of humanity. And just in time. In the fury to make a daily living and absorb the latest crush of world news and just get through it all, it's hard to remember what exactly it's all about.

People are "a little lower than God," Psalm 8 declares. (The King James Version says "a little lower than the angels.") And we're "crowned with . . . glory and honor." And we have dominion "over the works of your hands; you have put all things under [our] feet." We are deputies of the Creator, with a mandate to be worthy of the image of God.

In our better moments, we make music or philosophy or art or chocolate cakes. We nurture miracles of family life and charity. We coin words, keep score, try to do the right thing, and wrestle with conscience, strange dreams, commitments, pursuits of love, the question of God.

Commentators say Psalm 8 was performed at evening Temple worship, with special choirs lifting up their voices and the expanse of stars looking down. The Milky Way reminded people of their tiny place in the big picture, but the psalm reminded them that here on earth they had dominion, sponsored by a loving Almighty.

Today every new photo transmitted from the Hubble telescope pushes the known limits of the universe to new definitions of vastness. Human puniness continues apace. But feelings of insignificance more likely come from less-than-cosmic sources: society's little cruelties, people's put-downs and snobbish materialism, slights that take away self-esteem or fuel self-hatred.

"Crowned . . . with glory and honor"? Every time someone gets up the gumption to speak from the heart or make poetry of gratitude, the air swirls with human potential. The work of divine imprint has already been laid. Glory and honor are possible, within reach, a little lower than God, seconds away. Every time.

> *When I look at your heavens, the work of your fingers,*
> *the moon and the stars that you have established;*
> *what are human beings that you are mindful of them,*
> *mortals that you care for them?*

PSALM 9: *Zigzag*

You have destroyed the wicked;
*   you have blotted out their name forever and ever.*

Where does God reside? On a throne, forever, Psalm 9 says. God "sits enthroned" as judge, stronghold, begetter of righteousness. God is vivid, explosive, sudden, and near—an expectation projected into the heart of faith like a flickering image.

God rebukes the godless ones and destroys the wicked. Psalm 9 is poetry for God's victory. Yet the psalm's emotions zig and zag between marvel and dread. After a run of exaltations of God's victories, anxiety seeps in. The psalm makes a plea: "Rise up, O LORD! Do not let mortals prevail." The psalmist worries that mischief makers will make a comeback against God's designs.

Psalm 9 asserts a world where good and evil flourish in coexistence, and the triumph of good is a fragile, unpredictable thing. Those who disdain God have their own power base. Their physical power fills the room in its own way. The Lord, we are told, visits the meek and the afflicted, those who seek God. The arrogant carry along in defiance, free to do their damage, for now.

The psalm's zigging and zagging between emotional ups and downs has another explanation. The psalmist, writing in the original Hebrew, was having some intricate fun: Psalms 9 and 10, which were combined in an early Bible, the Septuagint, were written on an acrostic model, where successive lines begin with the next letter of the Hebrew alphabet. Themes jump around so that the work conforms to a consistent literary pattern.

Perhaps the world's unpredictability, the erratic weave of good and evil, will one day be revealed to contain its own ultimate and explainable pattern.

Put them in fear, O LORD;
*   let the nations know that they are only human.*

PSALM 10: *Boiling Over*

Why, O LORD, do you stand far off?
Why do you hide yourself in times of trouble?

W e're in new territory—rage. This is the angriest psalm yet, a furious lament about the injustices of the world, its evil and unfairness.

The psalm writer rails against the persecution of the poor, the devious plans of the arrogant, the boasters, the haters of God. He pleads, "Rise up, O LORD; O God, lift up your hand; do not forget the oppressed."

Psalm 10 asks why God allows such wickedness to run wild. It's not a comfortable psalm for organized religion. Official faiths give anger a short leash and scant permission. They fear that communal anger at God might leave a bad impression, upset the children, corrode the faith. Public worship always ends on a high note of triumphant hope. That's its mandate. Angry perplexity about the way the world is—the persistence of evil, the apparent silence of God—goes underground.

After raging about the successes of evil in God's world, Psalm 10 takes a different turn, declaring God is ultimately in charge and will take care of business: "O LORD, you will hear the desire of the meek; you will strengthen their heart."

The psalmist offers no simple explanations: Suffering and evildoing happen without good reason. Moments of faith burst in too without warning. God is God—how to explain that? By the end, the writer seems exhausted by the mysteries of earth and spirit and grateful to God nonetheless.

You will strengthen their heart, you will incline your ear
to do justice for the orphan and the oppressed,
so that those from earth may strike terror no more.

PSALM 11: *Violent Content*

The LORD tests the righteous and the wicked,
and his soul hates the lover of violence.

We're a religious nation, one of the most God-fearing on earth. Most Americans treat the Bible as the word of God. Yet we are also a violent nation. This dichotomy is a fearful mystery to foreign visitors who recoil in disbelief at our baffling combination of handgun ownership and Bible sales. On TV we watch *Touched by an Angel*—and *The Sopranos*.

The American soul contains few memories of gentle, nonviolent martyrs and heroes. Martin Luther King Jr. is our first official one. Our mythic mentors tend to be gunslingers and gangsters, bad boys who enjoy a reckless freedom from the burdens of citizenship and democracy. They equate murder and cruelty with transcendent liberty. Violence gets eroticized, commercialized, like sex. Violent images sell. The unthinkable becomes thinkable. We can't help but look at the screen without quite knowing why. Born and bred of market values, we seldom question an economic arrangement that glamorizes violence.

Violence is part of the American story, deemed a necessity for taming the frontier. Wild animals were slaughtered; Native Americans were slaughtered. Bibles packed for the pioneer journey contained paradoxical messages of peacemaking and violence. Alone under the big sky of the new world, the pioneers could wipe history away, break away the thin crust of civilization and start over. They found it possible to claim the will of God in the absence of religious institutions. In a radical way, murderers every day abuse this sense of freedom: They think they're playing God, playing out a delusion of absolute power in their own raging, resentful heads.

Unprecedented terrorism on American soil forced a rethinking of all sorts of priorities. The slaughter was all too real. The fashionable, commercialized violence of the movies was muted for a while.

God loves righteousness and obliterates wickedness, the Bible says. God will meet violence with violence, the divine prerogative. Such are paradoxes of heaven—and of America too.

On the wicked he will rain coals of fire and sulfur;
a scorching wind shall be the portion of their cup.
For the LORD is righteous.

PSALM 12: *Big Talk*

May the LORD cut off all flattering lips,
the tongue that makes great boasts.

On a recent flight, I overheard two strangers behind me engaged in an intense discussion of the Bible. Actually only one was doing most of the talking. He shared his faith, urging the other to trust the Lord to improve his finances and job prospects. He offered a torrent of advice, giving well-rounded answers in confident tones the entire two-hour trip. After landing, they parted. The talkative one strode off, satisfied he had again served God's will, though he hardly stopped talking long enough to learn the details and complications of the other guy's life.

There's a spiritual style in America—upbeat, bustling, ready with sports analogies and quotable answers. It borrows from the swaggering style of talk radio, as well as from the myth of the self-made man. It rides the conviction that phrases from scripture can be pasted onto life's questionnaire as the answer for every blank.

Next time the silent stranger on the plane might quote from Psalm 12. The psalm warns against speech that is too polished and smooth. Such speech signals trouble—vanity, deception, self-deception—a sign that the speaker will one day hit a brick wall of crisis when life throws a vicious curve and the pat phrases won't work anymore. It's an old story.

Psalm 12 suggests that God looks out for people who find themselves shut out from the glittering fast-talk culture: "'Because the poor are despoiled, because the needy groan, I will now rise up,' says the LORD."

We fondly and strategically quote the pure words of scripture. Indeed, Psalm 12 says the promises of the Lord are as pure as "silver refined in a furnace on the ground, purified seven times." But in God's eyes, the sighing of the needy gets the last word.

"I will place them in the safety for which they long."

PSALM 13: *Hurting*

How long, O LORD?
Will you forget me forever?

Whether in peacetime or war, griefs flow unabated. People hurt. Dysfunction in the city, the suburbs, and the countryside. Unspeakable plights that never make the newspaper—family rapes, corporate rip-offs, dating treacheries, mental sickness upon sickness, bank-breaking debilities the state won't pay for, physical ailments undiagnosed, terminal pain.

This is the ground Psalm 13 works. It's a cry from the depths—not in some literary way, like a poetic stunt, but in fever-soaked desperation: "Consider and answer me, O LORD my God! Give light to my eyes, or I will sleep the sleep of death."

The reader winces. But the griefs don't go away. Lately, they've reached critical mass in our society, perhaps in the name of therapeutic honesty or media saturation or the sheer weight of public danger and personal chaos.

Synagogues and churches that would never have considered such a service several years ago now host prayer services of healing, offering occasions for clergy's laying on of hands, anointing foreheads with oil, or giving worshipers a vocal opportunity to participate in public prayers and supplications.

A local clergyman started a healing service a few months ago. He didn't know if people would come, but they did. They packed the place. There was weeping and reconciliation between members. There was admission of wounds and brokenness. There was prayer like no one had ever seen.

Such unvarnished moments in public religion are impossible to predict. It took courage for a congregation to admit that the river of religious emotion includes currents of despondency and doubt—not secularized doubt but raw, frightening laments and screams inside the world of belief, the sort preserved in Psalm 13.

The psalmist moves from despair to hope in twenty-five short lines. It's a distance that millions of Americans are trying to cover every day.

Consider and answer me, O LORD my God!
Give light to my eyes, or I will sleep the sleep of death,

PSALM 14: *Atheist*

Fools say in their hearts, "There is no God."

Sometimes you meet an atheist. Not often, not in the South, not in America. But there are many kinds: some humble and engaging, others formerly religious and still mad about it. Or they keep a sense of humor about it all, still carrying on the quest for truth in a spirit of adventure. Others are quite evangelical about their unbelief.

In short, styles of unbelief, whether dignified or overbearing, do not differ much from those of believers: There are varieties of each. Force of personality will bend the rhetoric of belief or unbelief to its own needs. An aggressive extrovert doesn't stop being so because of conversion to atheism or Christianity.

In Psalm 14 the writer ridicules the ingratitude of those who refuse to believe. Yet by verse 2, the tables turn on believers too. The psalmist makes no distinction between believer and unbeliever. God looks out from heaven and finds everybody coming up short: "They have all gone astray, they are all alike perverse; there is no one who does good, no, not one."

Surprising news after hearing for an entire century that atheistic humanism was the mortal enemy of the world. Surprising to learn that the children of light are not automatically in hugely better spiritual shape than the children of darkness from the Almighty's point of view.

Meanwhile God is among "the company of the righteous." Until we get there, we're left to ponder the big boat we're all in, atheist and believer alike, the boat of mortality. Everybody sits here with the same needs of the refugee for nourishment and a home. Crammed in, drifting along, it's hard to tell the atheist from the believer.

There is no one who does good.

PSALM 15: *Preapproved*

Who may dwell on your holy hill?

Psalm 15 sounds pretty harsh. The entry requirements for abiding on God's "holy hill" include no oath-breaking, no backbiting, no money-lending at interest. Bankers and divorced couples seem marked for exclusion.

Well, not so fast. Scholars explain this is a roster of conditions for admission into Jerusalem's Jewish congregations at the time it was written. The clause against charging interest means rich believers shouldn't exploit their advantage over fellow believers. The rest of the slate of eight or nine items—against slandering and telling lies, for instance—more or less restates some of the Ten Commandments.

These days some new congregations market themselves to people who are sick of religious rules and churchy religion. One church down the road promotes a come-as-you-are style, making no demands on visitors of money or commitment, at least at first.

Such nondenominational congregations scarcely existed thirty years ago. Their secret to growth is to keep the demographics of their audience always in view, playing to people who've been especially bruised by life and are wary of judgmentalism and jargon from the pulpit. The sermons at these new-era assemblies aim to give the clientele some Bible lessons to get them through a tough week, along with a message they may never have heard before: God's mercy. They've already been preapproved.

Even a no-rules house of worship will have rules of its own. It's hard to reinvent the wheel, and pointless. When all is said and done, probably it won't differ much from all the older congregations that have relied on tried-and-true commandments some three thousand years old. The password into the place is *mercy*.

O LORD, who may abide in your tent?

PSALM 16: *Sufis*

I keep the LORD always before me.

It looked like a difficult assignment: to cover a rare local gathering of Sufis, members of a mystic Muslim tradition who chant, dance, and pray in a throbbing rhythmic circle. Then rush back on deadline to write about it.

That requires getting perfect strangers to stop what they're doing and talk to me. It means somehow penetrating their vocabulary, rendering fairly and accurately their rituals, passions, and the twelve-hundred-year history of their devotion—on deadline, in time for the next morning's newspaper editions.

As it turned out, the Sufis were gracious interviewees, inviting questions and giving access. It was an evening of slowly mounting chant, music, and body movement; a surge of ecstatic religious experience focusing on the ninety-nine names of God and calling God's presence down.

In such a tradition of mystical dance, the solution to wayward thoughts and distractions is to knock them all away with physical movement. The joy of the dance, framed by continuous prayer to God, crowds out verbal error and deviation from mind and heart. It argues that bodily movement is a conduit of holiness, not the seat of sin and depravity.

"Therefore my heart is glad, and my soul rejoices," Psalm 16 declares. "My body also rests secure."

Sometimes it takes a group of dancing Sufis to show a Christian what a Jewish psalm means.

You show me the path of life.
In your presence there is fullness of joy.

PSALM 17: *Deceit*

Give ear to my prayer from lips free of deceit.

Easter morning. The church was full, and I tried to speak and pray with lips pure and free of deceit, as Psalm 17 urges. It wasn't easy. So many people around, all wearing our Easter Sunday best, trying to look good, perhaps fishing for a compliment, hoping to see and be seen.

Despite the swanky swirl of fashion, it's still an hour of high sanctity. At worship, spiritual good feeling may arrive at any moment, the secret collaboration of mood, timing, and grace. Momentum carries the words of prayer or hymn-singing to new heights and speeds. Focus and conviction feel sharp, invincible. There's a wind at your back and clear sailing on the sea of worship. "I call upon you, for you will answer me, O God," Psalm 17 announces. "Incline your ear to me, hear my words."

Yet the goblins of self-righteousness are never far. Soon after church, I managed to have a regrettably impatient exchange with a bereaved woman who was just trying to drop off an obit about her father and didn't know whom to see. So much for my aura of sanctity.

The psalm says, "If you try my heart, if you visit me by night, if you test me, you will find no wickedness in me; my mouth does not transgress." Night is associated with stormy visitations, terrors, dark nights of the soul. The psalm beholds nighttime as an opportunity for divine clarity. The late-night quiet arrives as refuge and reckoning—no crowds, no TV blaring, no boss on duty, no conference calls. It's possible then to pay attention to the movements of your own thoughts, the heart's dreams and second guesses.

The quiet has a way of telling the truth or giving truth a place to land. The psalm then looks to morning: "As for me, I shall behold your face in righteousness; when I awake I shall be satisfied, beholding your likeness." It's time to seek honest words once more, wet the lips, and begin again.

Guard me as the apple of the eye;
hide me in the shadow of your wings.

PSALM 18: *King's Ransom*

You made me head of the nations.

A king wrote Psalm 18, perhaps King David himself, which explains its regal length. Kings had big stories to tell, tales of extravagant deeds that reinforced their authority. This king thanks the Lord for smashing his enemies and handing him victory. The tone is triumphant. The days of defeat, when psalm writers will plead to God for answers in the ruins, come later in the history of the 150 Psalms.

In ancient societies, the presence of the king made thoughts of God's majesty more real. God's authority sponsored the king's authority. People could imagine heaven as an extension of worldly governance, and it gave daily life a sense of grandeur.

At some point, however, kings were dethroned in the political history of the West. The sweep of human rights took away the monarchs' divine right, their benefit of the doubt as leaders of civilization, leaving only the doubt. Laypeople rose up to claim their own divine rights. The Protestant Reformation tried to strip away every mediator between heaven and the individual—king, priest, sacrament—whatever might separate a person from God. The removal of kings toppled an old symbol of human arrogance, the idea that one man could be the fully competent vessel for the hopes and ideals of everyone else in the realm.

Back in the 1930s, "Every Man a King" was the slogan of Louisiana governor Huey Long, and it got him elected. In modern democracy, each citizen is king or queen of his or her own little realm, the turf of ego, self-respect, personal possessions, everyone declaring independence. Authority is scattered, if not shattered. We rely on conscience and personal choice to be the wise monarchs of our conduct.

Some abuse the privilege, of course. They act the bully, insisting their wants perfectly mesh with the will of God. And the world suffers for it. It's a trade-off we've lived with since the death of kings.

It is you who light my lamp;
the LORD, my God, lights up my darkness.

PSALM 19: *Sun*

The heavens are telling the glory of God.

We don't hear many hymns to nature in church or synagogue, but here's one: Stars and sun speak for God's stunning handiwork in Psalm 19. The morning sun comes out "like a bridegroom from his wedding canopy, and like a strong man runs its course with joy."

Such extravagant praise of nature apparently made clergy professionals of the day panic when they saw this short text. It looked like a threat to orthodoxy. So, according to modern commentators, a biblical editor tacked on an unrelated sermon about religious law in hopes of diluting the poem to nature. The attempt clumsily doubled Psalm 19's length.

The same nervousness is seen today in the counsels of denominational life. Religious leaders don't care to see too much praise of nature: They worry that it slides quickly into pagan nature worship. A hymn to nature, celebrating the awe of the silent world beyond words, might also pose a challenge to the professionals who make their living by proclaiming words. Psalm 19 points to something real and accessible beyond doctrines of piety—sky, sun, earth, elements of the created world—and connects it to God's engineering as few Bible verses do.

For the last two hundred years or so, nature poets have been rebelling against church neglect of praise of nature. At the tail end of this tradition in English poetry stands Philip Larkin's poem "Solar," written in the mid-1960s. His post-Christian awe of nature salutes the inconceivable brightness of the sun hanging in "an unfurnished sky."

Larkin felt nothing for God, no thrill at the idea. His salute to the sun ends nowhere but in melancholy. Not so with Psalm 19, which rides a wave of joy despite the busy afterthoughts and good intentions of censorious biblical editors.

> *The heavens are telling the glory of God;*
>   *and the firmament proclaims his handiwork.*
> *Day to day pours forth speech,*
>   *and night to night declares knowledge.*

PSALM 20: *Just Ask*

Some take pride in chariots, and some in horses,
but our pride is in the name of the LORD our God.

The world of faith might be divided into two camps of people: Those looking to God as a super-involved deity who will find their lost car keys and get their house sold for a nice profit, or those who think it demeans and trivializes God and faith to ask for such things.

The first group figures God knows all—therefore, there's nothing too small that God can't do. The second group also figures God knows all— therefore, God knows our true needs and doesn't need to hear compulsive, self-serving requests.

Psalm 20 comes from a distant time. It's the voice of a king or military leader, or his stand-in, preparing for savage battle and pleading to God for help. The psalmist speaks from a position of great intimacy with the divine. It doesn't occur to him to refrain from asking anything of God. The speaker even pledges to put his army's faith in God, rather than military logistics.

There's much talk in our times about the difficulty of intimacy—divine, human, and otherwise. Some people are not burdened with such shyness: They give God credit for every victory of their NFL team.

Others are embarrassed to approach God that way: In a world where millions die in holocaust, war, and plague with their prayers going unanswered, they feel it insults the dead to ask God for something so trivial as a game-winning field goal.

Then there's the camp of earthlings who flinch at asking God any specific question that might trigger a specific answer, an answer we'd rather not face. That might be everybody some of the time.

The ancient Israelites didn't win every battle they fought. But they sought the divine answer in whatever outcome unfolded before them.

May he grant you your heart's desire, and fulfill all your plans.

PSALM 21: *Enemies List*

Your hand will find out all your enemies.

There's nothing very cozy or comfortable about Psalm 21, composed evidently in a climate of war. The psalm on behalf of a warrior king proclaims God's blessings on the monarch, then lashes out at enemies. God's on his side: "The Lord will swallow them up in his wrath, and fire will consume them."

Hatred of enemies spins a thread that runs through the Psalms. The reader must reckon with it—the wretched fantasies about destroying enemies, whether evil neighbors or national foes. It's perplexing to read. Nowadays, in our thermonuclear biohazard age, we're taught to seek reconciliation in the global village, to work for interfaith understanding and conflict resolution. Psalm 21 unleashes something that looks brutish and primitive: the use of God to justify one side's military aims against another. Who are these enemies? What's their side of the story? We never hear their prayers to God.

Psalm 21 is soaked in the terrible anxiety of a nation poised for battle. We don't know where God stands on the matter; God is not quoted.

Until recently, Americans found it easy to condescend or feel superior to the sentiments of Psalm 21 from our reportedly civilized vantage point. But now we know differently. The terrorist attacks shocked us into a new conflict. We got caught up in our own list of enemies, a list compiled in rage, ambivalence, confusion. We had little understanding of the other side. And both sides have brought God into the picture in ways that haven't been matched since the Middle Ages.

God calls for justice and mercy. The high drama of our time springs from the tragic tension between the demand for justice and the command of mercy, and from our not knowing how to choose between them.

The final verse of Psalm 21 eclipses the violent talk about enemies. The words exalt God, as if to release heavenly gold dust to settle on the dangerous human scene. I guess stranger things have happened.

> *Be exalted, O LORD, in your strength!*
> *We will sing and praise your power.*

PSALM 22: *Forsaken*

My God, my God, why have you forsaken me?

I f you're a Christian, it's impossible to read these quoted words without thinking of Jesus bleeding on the cross. The Bible attributes these words to him during his crucifixion.

For years it struck me as unlikely that Jesus spoke these exact words, as if in all his unbelievable pain he still had the inclination to quote specific passages from scripture. It seemed to lack psychological realism. Reading this passage now, I find it compelling to imagine that Jesus' intimacy with this psalm and others (notably Psalm 31) was such that they filled his dying need.

By Jesus' time, this psalm had been around for hundreds of years. It had a favored place among the ancient Hebrews as an intense expression of the soul's sweaty dreads and hopes. Maybe Jesus recited all of Psalm 22, but the Gospel according to Mark saw fit to quote only the first verse.

Our multitasking culture no longer knows much by heart. Personally, the list is a thin, paltry catalog accumulated over the years: "America the Beautiful" and "The Star-Spangled Banner," first verse; four-score and twenty pop songs, Beatle lyrics, and Sinatra show-stoppers; an hour's worth of old Protestant hymns; the series of computer keystrokes to get onto the Internet; a dozen phone numbers; a clutch of Bible verses; maybe two dozen poems. Does it all add up to a worldview?

Everybody carries around a secret mental scroll that could serve as an unofficial ultimate manifesto. If you were being buried alive, or dying peacefully in your bed, what final words would flood in?

The poor shall eat and be satisfied;
those who seek him shall praise the Lord.
May your hearts live forever!

PSALM 23: *Geography of Blessing*

The LORD is my shepherd, I shall not want.
He makes me lie down in green pastures;
he leads me beside still waters;
he restores my soul.

Psalm 23, the most famous psalm in America, travels to far places of mind, memory, and social need. These are often the last words on earth that a condemned criminal hears before facing the masked executioner.

If any psalm provides a little tabernacle of grace, this is it. Its pastoral images put you in a cool, lush, quiet, meadowy spot, some echo of an original Garden, a reminder that God's first encounters with the creatures of the earth were in the great outdoors, in the cool of the evening.

Everyday routine tends to deny these nature images—in the workplace, on the street, in religion itself. Technology pushes us further away from horizon and sky. The national parks restore a piece of it. So does baseball. The latest round of books on the spirituality of golf hints that the fairway is a gateway to pastoral wisdom.

The news delivered by this short psalm is as vivid today as twenty-five hundred years ago: Nature and nature's God offer restoration for the soul. The outdoor quiet, punctuated by bird sounds, breeze, and stream, harken back to the original world of Genesis, far from the clicking of the keyboard, the laugh tracks, and the engine backfirings. The first soothing images of God, the divine fingerprints, maintain vital association with nature.

Psalm 23 maps out a geography of blessing. The believer strolls through God's backyard, which is strewn with paths and valleys, and ends with a seat at a table in the house of the Lord.

Whether it's your last day on earth or your first, this psalm is one for a rainy day or a brilliantly sunny one.

Surely goodness and mercy shall follow me
all the days of my life,
and I shall dwell in the house of the LORD
my whole life long.

PSALM 24: *Grandeur*

Lift up your heads, O gates!
*   and be lifted up, O ancient doors!*
that the King of glory may come in.

People don't talk this way anymore. The music of our language usually
diverges from this sacred script. Psalm 24 shows what the language of
religious praise used to be. Such is the gulf between then and now. Most
books written on biblical religion in the last 150 years make note of this
disparity—how new thinking (evolution, therapy, physics) and news (disas-
ter, war, disease) have so crowded in on the psyche that we've lost conviction in the old words, lost the knack for them.

The Hebrews possibly chanted this psalm as they accompanied the ark
itself during ceremonial processionals—the ark of the covenant, the one of
legend and Indiana Jones movies, the portable carrier of the Ten Commandments. Somehow this psalm, like an ancient worship bulletin, survives from
that time. It carries with it a flash of something we didn't even know we
lacked—grandeur: "The earth is the LORD's and all that is in it, the world,
and those who live in it. . . . The LORD of hosts, he is the King of glory."

A brush with grandeur always feels ennobling. That's how you know it's
grandeur. Stirrings deep inside you open onto a larger vision than before. A
feeling of grandeur casts around for a fit language, words that fit the expand-
ing moment. A feeling of grandeur, wherever it might come from—a poem
by Yeats, a symphony by Schubert, a look into the Grand Canyon—makes
such language possible and necessary.

The words of this psalm still carry their glint after all these centuries.

Who is the King of glory?
*   The LORD, strong and mighty.*

PSALM 25: *Tender Mercies*

The friendship of the LORD is for those who fear him.

God is fearful. God is loving. Between these viewpoints organized religion is divided. Divine judgment, divine friendship—no congregation has quite figured out how to proclaim both with equal conviction or persuasiveness. It's hard for any church body or religious movement to stretch its arms wide enough to take in the entire Bible and emphasize all its teachings equally. Each takes one or two dominant threads and wraps its identity in that.

"Fear-based" religions, though much maligned, make a well-taken point: God is the all-powerful, fearful presence in the Bible, making creation out of chaos, blasting enemies into smoking heaps, presiding with absolute intensity at the Last Judgment. Yet they must contend with these words found in Psalm 25: "Be mindful of your mercy, O LORD, and of your steadfast love, for they have been from of old."

Meanwhile, congregations that promote God as absolute love and mercy deemphasize the theme of fear. They hold up a heroic vision of humanity's better nature, a story about our redemptive destiny in the Lord's hands. They do so by ignoring the more violent or mysterious actions of God, blaming instead the Bible writers' ideologies or corruptions of the text.

Fear makes an appearance in this psalm, fear serving as the only appropriate basis for a creature to approach the creator God. But the psalm then allows tenderness to outbid fear and leave its lasting impression: "All the paths of the LORD are steadfast love and faithfulness, for those who keep his covenant and his decrees."

Fear may course through the veins of the psalm writer, but fear alone cannot account for the shot of sweetness that reverberates here across the millennia of faith:

> *Lead me in your truth, and teach me,*
> *for you are the God of my salvation;*
> *for you I wait all day long.*

PSALM 26: *Walk This Way*

But as for me, I walk in my integrity;
redeem me, and be gracious to me.

I once saw a TV documentary on Buddhism, and it all came down to one unforgettable image at the end of the show—a robed monk pacing slowly, eyes closed. His head tilted slightly, bobbing in an attempt to obliterate all the illusions and obstructions of this life, all the restlessness and egotism, the aging and decay. His effort was epic, courageous, and likely doomed to failure on this earth.

That image dramatized the Buddhist version of walking with integrity on the arduous road to redemption, navigating the conflict between the material and the ethereal, between gravity and spirit. The skeptic will say the Buddhist way is futile, for how can anyone escape the body and the self, and still live? Yet every religion enters this struggle of spirit and flesh. Without the struggle, there is no religion.

Christians declare the Word made flesh, the triumph over death, the good news, the news of Easter day. We've been trying to settle how to go about that on the second day and the day after and every day ever since. That's the Christian struggle—how to live a Resurrection faith in a material world.

Everyone makes the walk, physically and metaphorically, in every moment of life, an attempt to embody a belief while moving forward in a powerful, hurting, aging body on a spinning planet. Psalm 26 notes the "walk" of integrity three times. The writer's task is to sing "aloud a song of thanksgiving" and arrive at "the place where your glory abides."

The psalmist will keep walking even if redemption doesn't quite fuse the molecules of body and spirit until somewhere on the other side.

My foot stands on level ground;
in the great congregation I will bless the LORD.

PSALM 27: *Gimme Shelter*

One thing I asked of the LORD,
that will I seek after:
to live in the house of the LORD all the days of my life.

Attendance is never huge at the little chapel, nestled in a large, down-town church. Sometimes my wife and I are the only ones there, facing the minister up front. (The minister commences the service no matter how many people come. The service is for God, he says, whether people show up that day or not.)

Under such conditions, you pay attention. You can't slouch. Your absent voice during the Lord's Prayer will be missed if your mind is wandering.

Elsewhere some worship sites draw five thousand, ten thousand, or more. The worship experience differs when attendance is three rather than fifteen thousand. In the smaller service, undistracted by 14,997 neighbors, you have room to notice details—the light in the stained glass, the intricate carvings at the altar, the homely little book of matches in the corner for lighting the candles. You notice the space you're in, the sacred proposition that's underway: The notion that the ornate room in the middle of a busy city is open to all for prayer and silence, standing against weather, traffic, and every social fashion for more than a century. The little place carries memories of the shufflings and piety of generations in their endless faithful comings and goings. The molecules stir with countless untold launchings of prayer.

Psalm 27 reads as if written by someone desperate for refuge in the Lord's house. That's where the seeker beholds beauty, strength, safety, the land of the living. Synagogue- and churchgoers know that feeling at worship time, the gratitude that the sanctuary is there at all to proclaim the story of God.

It's a place to wait for God and find oneself, packing wonder and courage for the road, which is located just on the other side of the aging, wooden sanctuary door.

Wait for the LORD;
be strong, and let your heart take courage;
wait for the LORD!

PSALM 28: *God Spoke*

To you, O LORD, I call;
my rock, do not refuse to hear me.

Every day people get out of their chair or pull off the highway or leave their job and sell the house because, suddenly, God spoke to them. That's how they explain the mysterious transaction that has taken place in heart and head: God spoke to me. In a religious nation, it happens all the time.

Other citizens find this puzzling. They hear only silence, the silence of God. Some learn to trust the silence as a divine sign of blessing, and they may go to some trouble to seek it out in monasteries or on mountaintops.

The God-spoke-to-me group has dramatic spiritual testimony to share, a rhetorical advantage. But the only known earthly test of validity is this: Do their lives and deeds bear good fruit?

What do people mean when they say "God spoke to me"? "God spoke to me" could mean any of the following:

- My conscience is speaking to me, the inner voice of morality.
- I've been gripped by sudden mysterious insight or motivation.
- I've discovered a metaphor (God "spoke" to me) that gives meaning to the course of my life or transforms my sense of vocation, a metaphor that animates gratitude and pursuit of faith.

Or "God spoke to me" could mean: God spoke to me.

Psalm 28 makes it seem natural to talk to God straightforwardly and expect to be heard. If communication with God is that easy, then divine silence may indeed be terrifying, a sign perhaps of disfavor.

Those who value God's silence or hear God only in the silence come to their wisdom differently—sometimes out of an experience of tragedy, a moment when God did not answer in any simple way, but the result is an experience of God in new and deeper dimensions because of their grief. They don't make the headlines, not in crowded spiritual USA. But Psalm 28 reminds us

Blessed be the LORD,
for he has heard the sound of my pleadings.
The LORD is my strength and my shield;
in him my heart trusts.

PSALM 29: *Tornado*

The God of glory thunders. . . .
The voice of the LORD breaks the cedars.

Except for those nimbus clouds and sunsets on Sunday school magazine covers, we don't often look to the weather to bring messages from God. The God of the Bible, we're taught, replaced the capricious, mythological deities who had haunted nature. The God we worship dwells in the heart and in the moral code of scripture, not in a sacred grove of trees and rivers at the summer solstice.

Yet many people never completely give up the feeling that God inhabits the earth, the very wind and soil. They talk of sacred places and sanctuaries, as if God is in this building or that one—in Chartres Cathedral, say, but not outside in the narrow lanes of the little French town itself. Or we declare God resides in the wafer, wine, and baptismal font. In a storm, when lightning explodes overhead, it's the closest we come to thinking we've run up against the anger of God: "The voice of the LORD shakes the wilderness."

A few years ago a tornado swept through town. Churches were conspicuously hit (the Protestant ones, anyway). I got anonymous calls from people who said the city was finally feeling God's wrath for the years of prosperous materialism, spiritual arrogance, adult bookstores, NFL football on the sabbath, and other sins.

The churches, shifting into emergency mode amid the rubble, offered a different story. The destruction forced them to be better believers, better practitioners of compassion to the many stunned people in the darkened neighborhoods. The storm had inspired fearful awe but only as God's creation always inspires awe. The storm brought an awful clarity that our routines and possessions are fragile and impermanent. People suddenly found God, not in the 150 miles-per-hour wind, but at work among neighbors cleaning up the shredded houses.

The LORD sits enthroned over the flood;
*   the LORD sits enthroned as king forever.*
May the LORD give strength to his people!
*   May the LORD bless his people with peace!*

PSALM 30: *Toy Story*

As for me, I said in my prosperity,
"I shall never be moved."

In the last decade we enjoyed the biggest prosperity run in American history, maybe in the history of the world. The Dow hit the stratosphere; McMansions chewed up the farmland; and spirituality was all the rage, a password as prevalent as dotcom and cell phone.

To a sociologist, the timing of this focus on spirituality was no coincidence. In the hierarchy of needs, the search for spiritual meaning begins after material well-being is secured. (Artists and prophets have always defied this, but never mind.)

Boil it down another way: We eventually tire of materialism. The more toys we have, the less they satisfy. The current wave of spirituality is the fruit of such disillusion.

Psalm 30 puts it this way: Prosperity leads to the puffed-up delusion of self-sufficiency. When that happened in the world of the Psalms, God hid God's face. It's a message scattered throughout the Bible: The prosperous don't think they need God. The number of passages about the spiritual dangers of being rich far surpass those about the hazards of being poor.

In America this is confusing news. People work hard and build affluence on the bounty of God's blessings. Material abundance feels like divine reward for hard work. But apparently a spiritual law of the universe moves in a different direction. Single-minded riches make people forget the basic facts:

- Everyone born is equal in God's sight.
- Everyone dies.
- Dying is not softened by the toys.
- Peace of mind isn't purchased with cash or credit.

In this psalm the writer has struggled mightily against illness. He recalls earlier days of health and prosperity when he gave little thought to God. In his recovery, he's learned a lesson; his gratitude lights up the sky.

For his anger is but for a moment;
his favor is for a lifetime.
Weeping may linger for the night,
but joy comes with the morning.

PSALM 31: *Chaucer*

Incline your ear to me;
rescue me speedily.

Without Psalm 31, the world of faith would be missing half its vocabulary for praying to God. Almost every verse has a phrase familiar to the poetry of piety:

- You are indeed my rock and my fortress.
- In you, O Lord, I seek refuge.
- Incline your ear to me.
- You have redeemed me.
- Deliver me from the hand of my enemies.
- Let your face shine upon your servant.
- Let the wicked be put to shame.
- The LORD preserves the faithful.
- Be strong, and let your heart take courage.

In the centuries before the Psalms, prayer and deities were local affairs. The Psalms universalized human spiritual longings and relief, taking the new romance with monotheism around the world. It's an audacious proposition to talk to the Almighty, speaking words in the dark to an inconceivable Creator, while hoping and believing that a redeeming answer will come in return.

The writer of Psalm 31 is like a Chaucer of the prayer life, an early word mapper of spiritual emotions for addressing God. The words flow like waves on the stormy sea, with treacherous dips and sudden heights. The psalmist testifies to a world of personal griefs—"I have passed out of mind like one who is dead"—but he thanks God for getting him through it all. The writer sees into secrets of divine goodness, hinting at heavenly geography and blessings to come: "Into your hand I commit my spirit."

I read Psalm 31 several times last night, letting its waves wash over and over. The lapping waves at the shoreline are a comforting sound, a way to drift off to sleep in an undertow of serenity, a shadow of divine protection.

Be strong, and let your heart take courage,
all you who wait for the LORD.

PSALM 32: *Sin*

Then I acknowledged my sin to you,
and I did not hide my iniquity.

*S*in is one of those words that always threatens to go stale from overuse, abuse, or neglect but then makes a comeback. Its staying power hinges on seeing in its hard little shell a nagging mystery. Part of the mystery is its sheer survival—outlasting the indignities and self-destructions of some of its loudest public promoters, the old-fashioned TV preachers. In our culture the word *sin* endures like a ruin sectioned off in the shiny suburbs, a notion in touch with silent antiquity and buried truth. But the strangeness of the word suggests a secret, an old clue that still illuminates our cracked human condition. To the psalm writer, sin was a hard-nosed fact of life, like the cold of winter itself. Packed into the word *sin* is the memory of a historical drama—a drama set in Eden with scenes of disobedience against God, followed by violent separation and banishment, then regret, restlessness, nostalgia, death, and the prospect of the journey back to paradise.

Religious history ever since has been a tug-of-war over definitions of sin. To some, sin is embedded in the flesh, in human frailty and miscue, in the heaviness of time, in all limitation, an error to be redeemed in God's new world. Others say sin means finitude, the creation itself, something to escape through whatever instant ecstasies lie at hand. Then there are those who deny sin exists at all: We are perfectible. Our mind's stumbling blocks can, with effort, be removed. Evil doesn't really exist. There is no taint, no smudge on humanity, except for the bad thoughts we allow ourselves to have or allow others to have about us.

Sin is the name of a play—part drama, part comedy—that we act out in the heart every day. All the elements of the story—paradise, disobedience, restoration—happen in a moody jumble, along with our attempt to understand it, overcome it, make peace with it, then go to sleep and wake up and face the drama again in the morning.

Happy are those whose transgression is forgiven,
whose sin is covered.

PSALM 33: *Hide-and-Seek*

The LORD looks down from heaven;
he sees all humankind.
From where he sits enthroned he watches
all the inhabitants of the earth.

Where is God? Each religion offers the answer, the goods, its own brand of God. Each has a rival signpost, rule book, songbook, formula, and glossary. God is in the heart or in the sweep of history or in nature or waiting in heaven.

Where is God now? In Psalm 33 God is watching. God watches "from the place of his habitation," says the King James Version. The news is this: God created earth, released goodness into the world, and continues to save souls. This is the vast logic of God's necessary invisibility. Only an invisible God can exist for an eternity, reside beyond all corruptions of time and physical being. Time and visibility wither. They are unsuitable vehicles for the ultimate God.

Agnostics say any notion of God is crippled by our hapless lack of knowledge. Atheists insist the whole thing is a fancy edifice of wishful thinking. Believers, meanwhile, build monuments, magnificent houses of worship, hoping to embody somehow the divine majesty. Eventually the marble will crumble; earthen vessels are not forever. Every empire and philosophy fades.

The Psalms point out the luscious, fatal temptation of the visible—the conceit of nations and ideologies to assume their own permanence. The reader is invited to reject that idea. The only permanent thing is the "counsel of the LORD," maker of all that is, seen and unseen. Praise, fear, awe, respect for God's moral code, celebration through music (that other invisible force) are the entry points of faith in the reign of invisibility.

Truly the eye of the LORD is on those who fear him,
on those who hope in his steadfast love.

PSALM 34: *Brokenhearted*

The LORD is near to the brokenhearted,
and saves the crushed in spirit.

R eligion's for old people," my buddy declared as we drove through the
countryside. His comment was a little insulting: I was a churchgoer,
age nineteen. Was that so wrong? Eventually I lost touch with him; now it's
been twenty-five years since we've spoken. But he was on to something. At
twenty, the road looks clear all the way to forever. We arrogantly waste time,
try a hundred new jobs or relationships or philosophies, believe any fool
thing. The heart is not yet broken, not in the way it is when time crashes
down on it—soured dreams, career missteps, divorce, illness, the death of
loved ones, the passing of so much we love. By old age the ghostly procession of the once-was can be unbearable.

My heroes include any elderly persons who keep the flame lit, who still
feel inspiration and outrage at ideas, current events, history, movies, books,
national tragedies, spring flowers, the passing parade. Somehow they take it all
in. Life enlarges their spirit, becomes fuel for the remaining journey, seasoned
with humor, not bitterness. They age with dignity. Part of the dignity is keeping the inevitable heartbreak framed by larger perspectives and by going
deeper into the grief, not denying it. The alternative is that other strategy of
the heart, the hardening of it.

In this age of AIDS and terrorism, poet Allen Ginsberg's words resound,
"It isn't enough for your heart to break because everybody's heart is broken
now." His observation sounded grandiose, pitiful, and true. Today's untold
longings and brokenheartedness are discovered in every new wave of spiritual quest and renewal, one of the biggest stories in America.

Sometimes I wonder what happened to my swaggering, young friend
who twenty-five years ago had no use for religion.

The angel of the LORD encamps
around those who fear him, and delivers them.
O taste and see that the LORD is good;
happy are those who take refuge in him.

PSALM 35: *Court Date*

Contend, O LORD, with those who contend with me.

Not everything in the Psalms is beauty and uplift. Psalm 35 embodies a voice of revenge, angry, pleading, sorrowful. It has the feel of a courtroom: "Bestir yourself for my defense, for my cause, my God and my Lord!"

We are asked to hang in there and hear the psalmist out. His speech, a mixture of the tiresome and the insightful, might make the reader wonder how this character found his way into the holy book. He rambles on like a real human being, like a friend torrentially unloading about his or her awful day. The psalmist complains of false witnesses, hypocrites, mockers. He asks God to confound his enemies and chase them away, to make them ashamed. Caught up in his own monologue, he doesn't say how he got into this fix or what mishap has befallen him.

Some preachers will try to spiritualize this psalm by saying the speaker's enemy is clearly Satan. Blame the devil. Yet Satan as an enemy of God and humanity wasn't always a clear concept in the Hebrew Bible. That came later, in New Testament times. So let us live with this troublesome psalm a little longer without explaining it away. Let us live with the biblical outburst of an actual person calling insistently on God for his own earthly reasons.

Many readers will want to glide over these emotional storms and get to the point, the sermon, the news we can use. But Psalm 35 tugs on our sleeve. The psalm writer won't stop until his name is cleared by God. He will have his day in court.

> *Let those who desire my vindication*
> *shout for joy and be glad,*
> *and say evermore,*
> *"Great is the LORD, who delights in the welfare of his servant."*

PSALM 36: *Grand Canyon*

Your righteousness is like the mighty mountains,
your judgments are like the great deep.

I happened to read Psalm 36 at the Grand Canyon. There's surely nothing more to say that hasn't been said already about the Canyon, one of the seven wonders of the natural world. Yet a hike on the narrow trails with this psalm's images echoing along invites a confrontation with a few brute geological facts and uneasy theological prospects.

The Colorado River in the Grand Canyon has been doing its stunning work of erosion and cliff-carving for more than one billion years. One billion. To venture up and down the trails, through clouds or sun, in daylight or pitch darkness, is to inhabit a prehuman, prehistoric silence and vastness.

Our convenient abstractions—a short little word like *eon*—evade the downright outrage of it all. The Grand Canyon, a mile deep and 277 miles long and in some places eighteen miles wide, serves as a corrective to any glib claim of human permanence.

It's uncomfortable to think that human praise of God is so recent, barely a second or two in geologic time. All was humanly silent—a billion years of silence—until mere thousands of years ago. No wonder antievolutionists want to say that the earth is just a few thousand years old. It's a bad blow to the human ego to think God did without us for so long. We were apparently not needed, not yet. Praise perhaps was offered by the caw of the raven or the whistling wind off a mesa or the bright reds of sunrise on the cliffs of the Canyon's North Rim. For millions of years.

Psalm 36 testifies to majestic divinity in fond, familiar words. They console; they bring us into the chorus of God's care. They also keep us from going crazy, allowing us to forget or lay aside the dizzying scale of majesty that the Bible announces—"your judgments are like the great deep." How inconceivable—even more so than the deeps of the Grand Canyon.

Your steadfast love, O LORD, extends to the heavens,
your faithfulness to the clouds. . . .
you save humans and animals alike, O LORD. . . .
All people may take refuge in the shadow of your wings.

PSALM 37: *Meek*

But the meek shall inherit the land.

I thought this verse originated with Jesus, but apparently it came from Psalm 37. Jesus knew the Psalms and cited them to memorable effect. He honored this thought in his Sermon on the Mount, a blessing on meekness, kindness, humility, lack of resentment.

Psalm 37 meditates on blessings that come with patient waiting. Patience is the virtue: Believe it or not, evil will pass away, so hang on. This is a psalm for the wee hours, when it's plausible to think for a while in the stillness about the power of meekness and waiting. By day it seems less plausible. The world spins on aggressive behavior, deal-making, tight schedules, and big talk—not meekness.

These days spiritual retreat centers exist to allow people to dwell longer on a virtue like meekness, even dedicate daylight workaday hours to it without distraction. There's one a few miles out of town here, Penuel Ridge Retreat Center, a place of hospitality on 125 acres of hills and trails. It's known for its gentle spirit, welcoming atmosphere, and interfaith values. People making their first visit often remark on the peaceful feeling of the land, like a special place destined to stand apart.

Joyce, the soul of Penuel Ridge, died in late 2002, saddening a large circle of friends and protégés. She founded Penuel Ridge with her husband, Don, in the early 1980s, and together they embodied its hospitable spirit. Joyce believed people need to take time in the great outdoors to discover what their souls and lives are really telling them. For years she stood at the front door, greeting and orienting the newest strangers to Penuel Ridge. She had a knack for seeing potential in everyone she met. She helped people bloom like the spring wildflowers on the ridge of the retreat center itself. Everyone who knew Joyce wanted to rise to what she saw in them.

Joyce's ashes will be scattered on the land she loved and envisioned as a place where the humane meekness hidden in each of us might discover its inheritance.

> *Be still before the LORD, and wait patiently for him. . . .*
> *Trust in the LORD, and do good;*
> *so you will live in the land, and enjoy security.*

PSALM 38: *Ill Wind*

There is no health in my bones
because of my sin.

By now, the laws of modern science—with their sensible explanations of germs and immune systems—have colonized our worldview for three hundred years. Nevertheless, when serious illness strikes, a voice still manages to whisper inside: Why? Why is God allowing this? Is God angry? "O LORD, do not rebuke me in your anger, or discipline me in your wrath," says Psalm 38. And God is praised when health returns.

Belief in a world of spiritual cause and effect lingers on. It's a powerful idea. It tempts us to associate vitality and good health with God-anointed leadership. It's easy to make an unspoken leap and think God blesses robustness and disdains the nonrobust.

But illness is everybody's theological problem, an inevitable part of the machinery of mortality. Even when health is good, this psalm reminds us that all may not be well. Forgetfulness, arrogance, and bad faith all keep us from getting a clean bill of health.

The psalmist's ordeal of illness strips him of all pretense of invincibility: "I am utterly spent and crushed; I groan because of the tumult of my heart. O LORD, all my longing is known to you; my sighing is not hidden from you." The human condition is laid bare; life is made plain—his (our) dependence on God, his (our) inability to carry on alone.

The great mistake of healthy people is ingratitude, if they carry on as if ill health will never happen to them and as if their days are not numbered and they're not dependent on the cosmic scheme of things.

An unplanned life change is one breath away.

O my God, do not be far from me;
make haste to help me,
O Lord, my salvation.

PSALM 39: *Uncle Leo*

LORD, let me know my end,
  and what is the measure of my days;
  let me know how fleeting my life is.

My Uncle Leo died recently, well into his eighties, after a lifetime as a western Kansas wheat farmer. He had a shy sense of humor, a streak of skepticism, and a sunburned face peeking out from under his faded cap in the relentless summer sun. A man of deep weather wisdom, mechanical know-how, and familial love, he stayed on the farm as a lifelong bachelor while the rest of the big family moved off.

Uncle Leo died on the D-Day anniversary, June 6, a day that recalled deaths by the thousands on a beach in France. He had reluctantly stayed home during the war, farming so the Allies could eat.

The writer of Psalm 39 asks a question with a modern ring to it: What's this life about and why so short? How long will I live? Wouldn't it be better to have a clue about the deadline?

Belief in God means belief that God, not we, has worked out the wisdom of our life spans, how death will come and when. The mind-boggling diversity in life—languages, ethnicities, species, insects, even religions—suggests God has ordained such. Diversity of death too—all its many unthinkable ways and timetables—is no less stupefying.

Psalm 39 admits exasperation about it all: "Surely everyone stands as a mere breath. Surely everyone goes about like a shadow." The psalmist, enduring serious illness himself, sets down the stone-cold fact of mortality with no triumphant trumpets to drown out the news. He never wavers from the conviction that God masters and directs the whole picture, all life and death.

We laid Uncle Leo in the country cemetery overlooking the wheat fields he plowed for seventy years. The Kansas wind, never ceasing, never withdrawing its narrative of the passing of things, seemed to deliver news that comes wrapped in Psalm 39.

Toward the end, the psalmist searches for the right tone of humility under the circumstances. All these years later, we're in the same position.

Hear my prayer, O LORD, . . .
  For I am your passing guest,
  an alien, like all my forebears.

PSALM 40: *Graham*

I have told the glad news of deliverance
in the great congregation;
see, I have not restrained my lips.

Not so long ago, evangelist Billy Graham came to town, leading a four-night revival service, one of his last big crusades after a historic preaching career that spanned more than six decades. People came to hear—more than forty thousand every night, seventy-two thousand one evening.

Each night felt like history was being made, an era closing out, a remarkable individual vision made good. From the press table on the field, I watched Graham closely every session. He had to be helped to the podium because of Parkinson's and other illnesses, but his preaching remained strong and steady. Now in his eighties, he never showed a flicker of doubt, never a yawn or wandering sign of boredom. Every night he pressed with the same message of now-or-never salvation—make the choice, act on the stirrings; you might never have this chance again, be sure of your salvation. The formula has always drawn criticism as the holdover product of a nineteenth-century religious style, the result of strident, isolated Southern Protestantism. Those reservations are put on hold when you face the man and see the wracked body and hear the unwavering words of the narrow way of hope and catch the compassion, framed by a legendary humility.

Graham offered no surprises to this largely white, homogeneous crowd. People know what they're getting when Billy Graham comes a-calling. From now on, it will be hard to read Psalm 40 without thinking of him. Graham, born in North Carolina in the early twentieth century, seems to have sprung from the days of the Psalms when simple words corresponded to huge biblical actions, human commitments, laments, and claims on the divine attention.

I have not hidden your saving help within my heart,
I have spoken of your faithfulness and your salvation.

PSALM 41: *Drummer Boy*

As for me, I said, "O LORD, be gracious to me; heal me."

B ack in the early 1990s, I took hand-drum lessons. I had wearied of beating on the dashboard during radio tunes. An internal rhythm needed an outlet. Probably I was looking to rhythm as a kind of healing after years of frozen emotions in the wake of divorce. The lessons didn't work out for long. The teacher wanted to talk about religion, not rhythm. It seems she needed a healing too. Preoccupied with severe theories of predestination and the uncertainty of her salvation, she needed to know her place in the scheme.

Other venues for drumming abounded in those days. The men's movement was in full bloom. Writing a news story about it, I hung out once with a dozen guys in a dark, abandoned church. They pounded on drums for an hour, a slow, thick vein of sound, before taking turns talking about whatever was on their minds. They were looking for a healing too. You could hear it in the rhythmic current, a kind of SOS to the spirit world, God's doorstep. The setting—an old wooden church, long abandoned—offered tempting symbolism: the old orthodoxies in retreat, leaving lonely people to beat out truth on crude drum skins in the dark.

Psalm 41 is not exactly about beating on drums. The psalmist yearns for healing, but he is probably on his sickbed, pleading to God for health. He hears enemies mocking his illness. He seeks a direct line to God to make matters better: "But you, O LORD, be gracious to me, and raise me up."

People embark on many kinds of healing adventures—homeopathic pills, mountain climbing, rock concerts—in hopes of easing the wound and closing the broken circle of mind, body, and soul. The guys in the drumming circle had felt burned by traditional religion and couldn't get back to that. Yet there they were in a church, creating intricate sounds, in search of they-weren't-sure-what.

Elsewhere the Psalms urge people to make a joyful noise unto the Lord with cymbals and other instruments. Nothing emphatically excludes homemade drums in an abandoned church building.

Blessed be the LORD, the God of Israel,
from everlasting to everlasting. Amen and Amen.

BOOK II

THE SECRET
Heart

PSALM 42: *Soul Survivor*

My soul thirsts for God,
  for the living God.

After the mid-1990s when the angel trend began to subside, commercial publishers found a new meal ticket—soul. New titles declared getting in touch with it, being good to it, feeding it with chicken soup. Soul became a new, nondenominational way to reach the individual consumer and talk about transcendence and meaning without controversy. You could find soul without much mention of the stickier issue of finding God. Soul became the centerpiece of a nonsectarian, stay-at-home religion—a concept for an overheated, too-busy-for-church economy. The news was not that soul might inspire us to change the world for God but that we had a soul at all.

Psalm 42 puts the soul front and center. Having been ill, the psalm writer cannot make a pilgrimage to Jerusalem. His situation devastates him: He'll miss out on the huge parade of spiritual renewal and community. He suspects the illness is a sign of God's displeasure. We find him in suspenseful conversation with his soul. He calls to his soul, the part of him that encounters God, to remain hopeful and be ready for the next divine appointment: "By day the LORD commands his steadfast love, and at night his song is with me, a prayer to the God of my life."

The dictionary lists a half dozen definitions of *soul*: the essence of life, a person's spiritual core, a spirit of integrity, the exuberance of African American music or performance. It's the inner spirit that is insulted by modern life's fast food and spiritual equivalents. In the psalm world, the soul is a place that waits for the movement of God, the place where "deep calls to deep."

As a deer longs for flowing streams,
  so my soul longs for you, O God.

PSALM 43: *Vitamins*

Why have you cast me off?

The voice of the writer from Psalm 42 isn't done. He still has the floor; his soul is still disquieted, his health apparently still at issue. The rousing, glorious pilgrimage goes on without him. Somewhere off in the background, oppressive neighbors or disbelievers are mocking his ill health, taunting his weakness or doubt.

Compare the psalmist's health-consciousness to ours. In a culture of vitamins, exercise, and war on tobacco companies, we have even mobilized prayer to serve the cause of health promotion. Prayer is good for mind and body, according to some much-publicized studies. Combined with regular worship, it can lower blood pressure, extend life, promote contentment. There's something briskly utilitarian about this news, as if prayer, one of life's great mysteries, is a new miracle ingredient to add to the daily aerobic workout chart of sit-ups and jump rope.

The psalm writer has no access to personal trainers. Prayer is a constant in his life, whether health is good or ill. And God is the source of all health, good or ill. Twenty-two hundred years ago, no antibiotics or pharmaceuticals as we know them existed, only home remedies and the mysterious movement of God. Theologically, ill health makes no sense to the psalm writer because sickness cuts a person off from praising God with the community. Why would God allow that? In a psalm of illness, his prayer is desperate and depressed. He prays for health so he can return to the main action in Jerusalem and get on with the main event of praising God.

Depression doesn't get the last word. The psalm writer already makes plans for his recovery, God willing, multivitamins or no.

Then I will go to the altar of God,
   to God my exceeding joy;
and I will praise you with the harp,
   O God, my God.

PSALM 44: *Superpower*

Yet you have rejected us and abased us,
and have not gone out with our armies.

In ancient Israel, the fortunes of war came down to God. God decided who won or lost. People experienced victory or surrender as a sign of miraculous divine favor or gut-wrenching disfavor. Facing defeat, people complained not to the media but to the Almighty. They wanted to know why God had abandoned them. Psalm 44, soaked with national soul-searching and military setback, pleads to the Almighty, "Rouse yourself! Why do you sleep, O Lord? Awake, do not cast us off forever!"

Today politicians, lobbyists, and Sunday-morning TV pundits do all the explaining for us when war looms. Factoring God into the discussion is considered unseemly: Theology has no place in a superpower's foreign policy.

Until recently the last serious American public rhetoric about God's role in a conflict of war was the Civil War—Lincoln's Second Inaugural Address comes to mind. Public life still marched to biblical cadences that echo in psalms like this. Since then, of course, the latest guided missile system, not the King James Version, has been the yardstick of military success. When we lost in Vietnam, no one suggested (publicly) that God had sided with the opposition—godless communism in Buddhist Southeast Asia.

After the terrorist attacks on America in the new century, religion suddenly injected itself in public life and geopolitics. Worship attendance climbed. Jittery Americans consoled themselves to discover that the Bible had deep acquaintance with national crisis and personal suffering. The Psalms, no longer distant or theoretical, became a script of the real.

Psalm 44, a catalog of defeat, a tug-of-war between despair and hope, refuses to whitewash. In the new millennium, Americans willing to look found psalms like buried treasure, a dig forced by unforeseen ordeals, creating emotional alliance with a biblical people across forty centuries.

For we sink down to the dust;
our bodies cling to the ground.
Rise up, come to our help.

PSALM 45: *Wedding Announcement*

Grace is poured upon your lips;
therefore God has blessed you forever.

People pay lip service to the Bible all the time. Some proclaim that all of the Bible is holy, authoritative, without error: None of it's true unless all of it's true. Even so, we ignore vast portions of scripture every day.

Psalm 45 isn't the best-known psalm in the book. It's written as a flattering toast made by a court scribe to a king at his royal wedding. The king is so important that he is apparently called "God" in verse 6, which would be unprecedented in scripture.

The psalm uses tender language here and there, but the reader will have to look hard to find much spiritual excitement. The lesson perhaps is that the Bible is not just about us after all: In the wide net cast by the psalm collection, some miscellaneous themes turn up—this one, for instance.

One interesting note is the fierce irony of the ending—"I will cause your name to be celebrated in all generations." Today no one remembers who this king was. Time has wiped away the name of this "god," who now stands as anonymous as any serf or slave or peasant or the billions yet unborn. You can almost hear the dusty, mocking wind sweeping along, eroding every monument to royal and human vanity.

The sweep of scripture across the eons, which judges all human endeavor, scolds even the psalmist in this instance, a staff scribe of the court who excitedly exalts a monarch who turns out to be all too human, now forgotten.

Your throne, O God, endures forever and ever.

PSALM 46: *Quiet, Please*

Be still, and know that I am God!

After psalms of imperial pomp and complaints against enemies, now comes a sudden change of scenery, a pastoral vision of peace: "There is a river whose streams make glad the city of God." And then, like lightning: "Be still, and know that I am God!"

The command stands as a jolting spiritual motto that cuts against a modern grain. Be still, be quiet? Fear of silence is a national phobia. Some of us could talk nonstop about silence. Even believers discover this ill-at-ease feeling when they get away for a long-awaited spiritual retreat, only to find a boiling river of emotion welling up from the silence after years of inattention.

I've known it myself. Visiting a monastery in Kentucky, I discovered after just a few hours of (enforced) silence that every repressed and forgotten fear or hope rises up to demand attention. There was no escaping it. Always bring a notebook and a sense of adventure to such an outing.

"Be still, and know that I am God!" This simple advice carries a hint of reproach. All the familiar intermediary steps to stillness—the gurus, the self-help bestsellers—momentarily stand aside. The psalm asks the believer to rely on no props, only humility, to make a new start. This God claims domain, like no one else, over life's very molecules.

The stillness provides a foretaste of an inevitable ultimate stillness: death, when the final encounter with What Awaits takes place, according to the organized faiths.

Being still is a dress rehearsal, a practice session. Practice makes perfect.

God is our refuge and strength,
a very present help in trouble.
Therefore we will not fear, though the earth should change,
though the mountains shake in the heart of the sea.

PSALM 47: *All Together Now*

Clap your hands, all you peoples.

This is the explosive beginning of Psalm 47—a scene of praise singing, instruments, clapping. It sounds like a hootenanny; a Friday-night revival, vividly detailed and human, with real people stirring out of their seats and off the floor.

Freshness doesn't always come through in Bible reading. Characters in Bible stories can get a bit out of focus, overshadowed by the storms of God's mighty acts, or they move in slow motion without facial expression like Sunday school cutouts. It's hard to see the laughter or the tears.

Not this time. The celebration is a thunderclap. You can almost see the worshipers sitting in their places, under roof or sky, fidgeting, eager; singing praise to the world-altering conviction that God stands over their history. Trumpets and shouts fill the desert air, the awesome stage of faith. And you can imagine everybody going home afterward to stone shelters or realities of dirt or danger with musical praise of God still ringing in their ears and prayer creating an almost physical connection to divine realms: "For the shields of the earth belong to God; he is highly exalted."

And you wonder if, for this scattered assembly of believers, the shine of the worship moment lost a little luster the next day as a thousand preoccupations flooded back into mind. Even so, you realize that real people in spite of it all found themselves living out a story of miracle and song that would one day become nothing less than Holy Scripture.

For God is the king of all the earth;
*   sing praises with a psalm.*

PSALM 48: *Old Fogy*

. . . that you may tell the next generation
that this is God.

I t's a national pastime to write off the present generation—the boy bands, the tattoos, the green hair. Old fogyism is a perennial theme, a midlife complaint as old as the hills. In my mid-forties, I'm fighting the latest round with the fogy within, trying to comprehend and survive the hyperventilating media stream of the moment, which, as of ten minutes ago, was obsessed with images of Britney, J. Lo, and Eminem.

Organized religion perpetually does battle with that part of its nature, the overcareful fogyish part. One minute there's a gray-haired despair at the reckless blankness of youth culture; the next minute a suffocating embrace of all the kinetic noise of MTV, with baggy pants in the pulpit, hip-hop pastors, fog machines at the altar.

Even in the ancient days of the Psalms, so close to the foundations of revelation, even then the people worried. They had no guarantee that the next generation would get it. Bringing the faith forward takes work, patience, and a feeling of stewardship both for ancestors and unborn descendants.

"He will be our guide forever," Psalm 48 says. The words cut through the arrogance of every generation, which always thinks there's no guide for its unique discoveries. Anxiety-ridden adolescence is a terminal condition that will disappear as youngsters make their way to the land of grown-up perceptions, hopefully with mind and body intact and also with as little bitterness as possible.

From the viewpoint of forever, youthful swagger and old fogyism are two sides of the same coin, the coin of fond self-absorption. It's up to us fogies, who should know better, to bring our own elder energies to the table and let the kids know that the old faith—well-trod, battle-tested, good-humored, not easily fooled—is theirs to get them through the next sixty minutes, the next sixty years.

As we have heard, so have we seen
in the city of the LORD *of hosts,*
in the city of our God,
which God establishes forever.

PSALM 49: *Grave Logic*

Mortals cannot abide in their pomp;
  they are like the animals that perish.

According to the cynic, organized religion exists to reassure the paying customers that they will live forever. Yet biblical references to the afterlife are rather meager; there's no consensus about what exactly happens when we die.

Our most popular assumption says we are immediately judged at death and dispatched to heaven, hell, or purgatory. Or, our immortal souls wait indefinitely in silent, gravelike repose until the coming (or return) of the Messiah and the final Judgment Day. Or, according to a third view popularized by near-death-experience testimonies, the warm light of deity welcomes us all on the other side.

This psalm hovers over grim realities of the grave without much reassurance. It aims to soothe a fear of the rich and powerful by reminding readers that all die equally—the wise, the foolish, the rich, the unknown. The grave is everybody's destination. Everyone perishes like an animal.

The psalm offers also the hope that "God will ransom my soul from the power of Sheol," the shadowy afterlife in the Hebrew Bible. Absent is the vocabulary of heaven and hell and resurrection that comes later in the biblical story.

The lack of sentimentality makes Psalm 49 all the more remarkable. Its bleak tenor and ridicule of wealth pretty much disqualify it from any modern-day list of most popular psalms, at least in public worship. Try it at home instead. After a long day it has a strange ability to console.

My mouth shall speak wisdom;
  the meditation of my heart shall be understanding.
I will incline my ear to a proverb;
  I will solve my riddle to the music of the harp.

PSALM 50: *Soul Travel*

Offer to God a sacrifice of thanksgiving.

The Bible gives the impression that the soul—the inner life, the drama of conscience, the spark of personal transcendence and destiny—emerges only gradually in the history of faith. God's redeeming actions turn to the canvas of the human inner world in the fullness of time.

Psalm 50 brings this theme to bear on animal sacrifice. God eventually wearies of such sacrifice: "For every wild animal of the forest is mine, the cattle on a thousand hills." If the animals already belong to God, why sacrifice them to God? God wants something more difficult than the slaughter of a barnyard animal. God wants commitment from the inner life—prayer and thanksgiving and every troubled confession. The garden of the human heart becomes the new harvest field.

The conflict between the religion of externals and the religion of the heart plays out every day. For some people a sacrifice of money or weekly worship attendance comes easier than confronting the heart's dark corridors. The psalm pleads for a rich interior life, a rejection of ulterior evil, a pursuit of holiness and discipline, not mechanical worship.

At the end of Psalm 50, God is still God, with the divine prerogative to act whenever and wherever, whether in the soul's garden or the larger world. Ignoring God has cosmic consequences for both the externals and internals of faith.

> *But to the wicked God says:*
> > *"What right have you to recite my statutes,*
> > *or take my covenant on your lips?*
>
> . . . .
>
> *"Those who bring thanksgiving as their sacrifice honor me;*
> > *to those who go the right way*
> > *I will show the salvation of God."*

PSALM 51: *Homeland Security*

The sacrifice acceptable to God is a broken spirit;
   a broken and contrite heart, O God, you will not despise.

I visited ground zero in Manhattan a couple of months after 9/11. A dense wall of faded flowers, scrawled prayers, biblical warnings of Armageddon, and photos of victims lined the perimeter of the destruction. Onlookers slowed down, watching their step, keeping a respectful distance from the individuals who had serious business here, those who were kneeling and weeping.

Ground zero is a mass grave, an absence. Nearly three thousand people dead or missing. Looking up, you could see the awful skyward blankness where the two towers used to be, now open sky, a shaft of invisibility stretching to infinity.

In an instant lower Manhattan became an obscene terminus for life-hating rage. In the same instant it launched a new war, far-flung and far-reaching. Normal words and ways of communicating don't work well in such a place. If anything, ground zero is a zone emptied of words. Only tears, silence, courage beyond words, bear up to it.

As a nation we are casting off the stoicism of our forebears under the pressure of events. The new century is producing new magnitudes of sorrow. After the Oklahoma City bombing, after the Columbine school shooting massacre, after the terrorist attacks, a need for public expressions of pain and the consolations of faith burst through.

The fragile state of human life is there for all to see, a vulnerability everyone shares despite posturings of invincibility. The new attitude eclipses the previous generation's public emotional reticence. It is breaking organized religion of its emotional reserve every day.

Heartbreak, war, and rumors of war—a new reign of public ordeals—touch every family. Psalms of anguish and hope, like familiar Psalm 51, get a fresh and urgent hearing.

Create in me a clean heart, O God;
   and put a new and right spirit within me.

PSALM 52: *Mainline*

But I am like a green olive tree
in the house of God.
I trust in the steadfast love of God forever and ever.

Psalm 52 is a broadside against words that deceive and devour, the slick plots of mischief that "love evil more than good." The good belongs to those who trust in the divine love and ride out the bad times.

I heard this psalm read in a mainline Protestant church, a place of worship in the central city, where it has served people and neighborhoods for more than a century. The words fit the place and time. "I will thank you forever, because of what you have done. In the presence of the faithful I will proclaim your name, for it is good."

For thirty years it's been fashionable to sneer at mainline congregations and the very idea of denominationalism: They're too liberal, too bureaucratic, too old-fashioned, too slow. This self-serving argument, tirelessly promoted by professional pessimists, expresses contempt for consensus politics and interfaith tolerance. It dazzles the media.

For better or worse, mainliners—a wide range of Protestants, Catholics, and Jews—are by instinct moderates. They aren't so keen to join the fractious fray and wars of words. They have work to do. Mainliners are an unsung demographic: They are nurturers of civic sanity in a contentious time. They aren't taken in by hysterical theories of national decline. They remain suspicious of blowhards, ruinous economic schemes, and radical prime-time rhetoric. They go about their lives pitching in at soup kitchens, volunteering at shelters, giving money and time. They do good deeds and get little credit, nor do they ask for it. They'll still be here long after their critics exhaust themselves and change careers.

All day long you are plotting destruction.
Your tongue is like a sharp razor,
you worker of treachery.
You love evil more than good,
and lying more than speaking the truth.
You love all words that devour,
O deceitful tongue.

PSALM 53: *Atheism, the Sequel*

Have they no knowledge, those evildoers,
who eat up my people as they eat bread,
and do not call upon God?

S ometimes psalms repeat themselves. Psalm 53 strongly resembles Psalm
14. The writer expresses disgust with the unbelief of his time. Whatever
the scholarly reasons for the duplication, the psalm editors decided the message bore repeating: Atheism is foolish. Another lasting impression is this:
Believers aren't automatically in the membership of the righteous, for
everyone falls short of seeking God.

Atheism is still a scary word in this country. We want separation of church
and state—but not too much: It's hard to imagine voters electing an outspo-
ken unbeliever as president. Nevertheless, atheist groups have become more
assertive than ever about the morality of their philosophical position. They
point to the high ethical standards of freethinkers, their intellectual honesty,
their courage to face the great human dread—death—and declare that nothing can save us except rational thought.

Atheism is not confined to atheists. There's such a thing as a functional
atheist—yes, even in church—one who claims belief in God but lives as if he
or she doesn't. Some churchgoers believe the world has deteriorated so badly
that the devil's in total control. They credit Satan as being the most active
force in the world, not God. Anti-Semitism also denies the God of scripture,
as does a willful ignorance of the Ten Commandments. Celebrity worship,
awarding pop stars godlike magical powers to enchant the world, demotes the
biblical God. So does hoarding money or a craving for miracles if it betrays a
lack of confidence in the power of faith to get a person through the day.

Psalm 53 recommends regular self-reassessment. For believers, it's still
a little early for self-congratulations.

God looks down from heaven on humankind
to see if there are any who are wise,
who seek after God.

They have all fallen away, they are all alike perverse.

PSALM 54: *Providence*

But surely, God is my helper;
*   the Lord is the upholder of my life.*

Recently Tennesseans voted to allow legalized gambling in the state. Tennessee was one of the last states to be without some form of gambling; the Protestant churches had kept it at bay. But this time no one could muster enough moral outrage to turn back the lottery.

Theology doesn't get debated much in public life, but that doesn't mean the tectonic plates of collective belief aren't grinding and shifting underfoot. By the early twenty-first century, society was undergoing a theological shift—from a belief in providence to reliance on luck.

Games of luck and chance—casino blackjack, lotto, video poker—have become a matter of public policy. It's a cheap way for politicians to raise public funds in an era that preaches contempt for government and taxation. And citizens buy into it, a dollar at a time. The fantasy of striking it rich with a lottery ticket lends excitement to daily routine and excuses us from tending to any other vision of national values or a safety net of social services. A nation of gamblers enshrines losing as a national pastime. It also nurtures the nervous, white-knuckled hope that tomorrow will bring the jackpot—for me, that is, not for you.

Belief in providence is the great inheritance of biblical religion, and the most nerve-wrackingly mysterious. Providence infuses the Psalms, surfacing momentarily in Psalm 54: "But surely, God is my helper; the Lord is the upholder of my life." The will of God renews daily a covenant with the universe, unfolding a plan that has a slot for everybody, though nobody can ever quite put a finger on it.

Luck wakes up every morning trusting nothing but a wishful feeling in its bones. Belief in providence seems to require the opposite. It implies trust, the trust that all shall be well, and nothing is a crapshoot.

With a freewill offering I will sacrifice to you;
*   I will give thanks to your name, O LORD, for it is good.*
For he has delivered me from every trouble.

PSALM 55: *Watching Friends*

It is not enemies who taunt me—
. . . But it is you, my equal,
*   my companion, my familiar friend.*

The subject of friendship doesn't come up much in the Bible. Two of the most famous passages include the relationship of David and Jonathan and the words of Jesus that "no one has greater love than this, to lay down one's life for one's friends" (John 15:13).

When friendship shows up in a psalm, I wonder what it meant in 500 B.C.E. What did friends do together? Were friendships restricted by class, income, ethnicity? Could men and women be friends? Did men have trouble making friends? Psalm 55 speaks to the betrayal of a friendship. While the details are hard to piece together, a friend has abandoned the psalm writer, and it hurts so much that he wants the friend blasted by God.

It's jarring to experience the falling away of an old friendship that has run out of steam, the unhappy result of changing priorities, ill-conceived comments, misunderstandings, impatience. This psalm's emotion seems excessive—blast the former-friend-now-enemy, "Let death come upon them." All bridges to reconciliation have been torched and charred, made uncrossable. Patching it up looks unlikely: "The words of his mouth were smoother than butter, but war was in his heart" (KJV). The sting, sorrow, and treachery of a broken-down friendship cut deep.

Friendships are priceless and life-giving. They are also fragile. Realize what you have. Stay in touch.

Cast your burden on the LORD,
*   and he will sustain you.*

PSALM 56: *Undying Words*

For you have delivered my soul from death.

I studied religion in graduate school a couple of years, a fine time of thick books, long walks, and no money. This was during the last embers of the 1970s, an innocent season before America was remade in the cauldron of the next decade's big money, shiny bistros, and biotech revolutions.

Every day we students met new people in the easy commerce of grad school camaraderie, sharing common intellectual goals and material miseries. A conspicuous presence was the smiling personality of Richard, who had a way of citing heroes like Martin Luther King Jr. and Dietrich Bonhoeffer and startling people with mottos for life, such as, "Until you find something to die for, you won't have something to live for" or "Today is a good day to live, a good day to die."

Richard was young (we all were), and his exuberant talk might have been no more than a dress rehearsal for the real world. But we envied him: He had found an organizing principle for his life. His aphorisms upheld a staggering paradox: Death is central to the meaning of life. Awareness of death, knowing the finiteness of life, gives life its zest. If you're fearful of death, you'll also be fearful of life. Finding the right attitude toward mortality will launch an authentic journey into life.

Psalm 56 plays with the same paradox—"In God I trust; I am not afraid; what can flesh do to me?" The psalm writer appears to be unafraid of death. He trusts God to guide him in the "light of life." He seeks communion with God, who knows all the birthdays and death dates and whose perspective swallows up both life and death.

I don't know how Richard turned out. I hope he's still riding the paradoxes of life for all they're worth.

> *In God, whose word I praise,*
> *in the LORD, whose word I praise, . . .*
> *What can a mere mortal do to me?*

PSALM 57: *Soul Power*

For in you my soul takes refuge;
in the shadow of your wings I will take refuge,
until the destroying storms pass by.

Soul was a big word in the 1960s and '70s—soul music, soul food, Soul Train. The word swept into the vocabulary to give voice to black music and experience, part of the new empowerment of African American culture. Then came the "soulless" 1980s, followed by the 1990s, when soul made a comeback, sporting a makeover. Soul bestowed authenticity on everything from Gothic cathedrals to Delta blues to Italian meals. Soul was a backlash against latter-day inflated résumés and infomercials. It became a byword for the search for personal faith. Soul became synonymous with spiritual liberation, a counterattack on a world of junk bonds, junk mail, junk food.

In Psalm 57 the word *soul* shows up three times—always the soul seeks God "in the shadow of your wings," away from the soul's damaging enemies. The soul is that part of human experience that awakens to God through music, thanksgiving, discipline.

How do we explain these mysteries? We flail about for metaphors. Maybe the soul is a silent air balloon that reaches into the high, clean air of the divine. Maybe the soul is the internal airstrip God uses to visit us. Well, maybe.

The storehouse of religious images gets stretched to the limit in times of unsurpassed prosperity and sudden insecurity. It's the job of the public connoisseurs of inspiration—pastors, poets, politicians—to forge new metaphors or rediscover the old ones and awaken the soul's place in the scheme of things.

In Psalm 57 the soul gets bruised, but it pleads for God's mercy and finds the words, hoping that today will be the day:

Awake, O harp and lyre!
I will awake the dawn.
I will give thanks to you, O Lord, among the peoples.

PSALM 58: *Nonnegotiable*

Do you indeed decree what is right, you gods?
Do you judge people fairly?
No, in your hearts you devise wrongs;
your hands deal out violence on earth.

In some translations Psalm 58 addresses gods plural, the old gods of the world, blaming them for doing violence on earth. The psalm writer disdains such heathen gods. They are unworthy of worship. They plot mischief and deserve vengeance.

In mythologies of old, the gods quarrel and put obstacles in people's way. It's a crowded field of these gods. From the psalm's point of view, they never did a good job of inspiring human trust. Instead, people tried to bargain with them, steal their thunder, hack into the database of their power.

The psalm shifts all power and wonder to the one God, the author and judge of all history. The monotheistic idea clears the field of other gods, their cliques, and their politics. With the one God, there's no negotiation, only grace, judgment, faith.

Nevertheless the old polytheistic instinct that served for so long still lives in religion today among professed monotheists whenever people try to bargain with God. Critics dismissed the recent angel craze in pop culture as a polytheistic outbreak of belief in deputized second-order spiritual beings.

Monotheism cut down the spiritual obstructions to present a clear view of the horizon. One God in control. Everyone else's job comes down to a simple, hard demand—doing right.

People will say, "Surely there is a reward for the righteous;
surely there is a God who judges on earth."

PSALM 59: *Haunted*

Each evening they come back,
howling like dogs
and prowling about the city.

Friday the 13th comes later this week. I can feel a mental softening coming, a jokey acceptance of the rules of the game of superstition. We look for trouble that day. Look for trouble, and you'll probably find it. Fret about being accident-prone, and you'll likely trip over the broom and break the good china.

Not long ago, I got spooked by the movie *The Blair Witch Project*. For a couple of days, my head swarmed with a haunting enemy, a fear of unknown entities invading the house or the backyard at night when forces from the unconscious famously rise up to do battle against one's better nature. When a light fixture in another room fell to the floor and shattered at midnight (of course), it felt like the evil entities had upped the stakes indeed. The world seemed lousy with bad spirits, crowding my own faith out of the picture. The spiritual vertigo was real.

By the clarifying light of morning, my frozen fears began to thaw. It had all been in my head—the fear, the self-involved fright, the will-o'-the-wisps that I ostentatiously projected as universal truth.

I managed to think my way through to my right senses again. It's true that the light fixture had shattered that night, but it's also true that I had improperly installed it weeks before. Reading a psalm in such circumstances serves as an antidote to the vertigo. The words of the psalm feel solid, with roots thousands of years deep. They stand like columns of fire on nervous nights, flickering through the scares and scars of the centuries, a light to the countless, nameless passing souls until morning can arrive to illuminate creation again.

But I will sing of your might;
I will sing aloud of your steadfast love in the morning.

PSALM 60: *Wine of Astonishment*

O God, you have rejected us, broken our defenses;
you have been angry; now restore us!

This could be the theme psalm of the South, at least the Old South. That's how it felt after the Civil War—a cosmic rejection, God's abandoning the cause. Defeat unleashed generations of guilt, scapegoating, self-defeat, and classic literature.

Defeat also intensified the region's stewing religious identity. Like a recessive gene, the tired-out revivalism of the early 1800s came to life again. Feeling the shame of losing a war, many Southerners were now determined to be winners in the denominational competition of salvation and the harvest of souls.

(As a Southerner and college football fan, I've often wondered if the region's love of the gridiron is no coincidence. Football, like a morality play, satisfyingly reduces life to plain action and its consequences, good guys and bad, victory and defeat, revealed by a glance at the scoreboard. There's a keen interest in being on a winning side.)

America itself carries on a preoccupation with religion (and football). We don't carry long memories of European or African ancestry, glory and sorrows. Here, we're determined to fly above tragedy's gravitational force. The New World meant escape from sad, old Europe and the burden of history. We're blessed with freedom and open sky and founded on abstract concepts of liberty, but the whispered American question never quite went away: Who am I? Religious intensity is a form of identity.

Then came the terrorist attack on our own mainland, the worst domestic carnage since the Civil War. Reading Psalm 60 was a new experience: "Thou hast shown thy people hard things: thou hast made us to drink the wine of astonishment" (KJV).

Psalm 60 closes with a plea for strength on the field of daily battle, where everyone takes turns winning and losing.

O grant us help against the foe,
for human help is worthless.

PSALM 61: *Foul-Weather Friend*

From the end of the earth I call to you,
when my heart is faint.

Two verses jump out and sink in time after time. The first is quoted above: "From the end of the earth I call to you, when my heart is faint." We have a duty to sweat the theological details of this business of living. But life isn't always so starched and organized. The hurricane of religious feeling always precedes orderly thought. The cry of prayer from despair or gratitude doesn't wait to get all its intellectual ducks in a row first. The dead-serious outburst to God doesn't wait for the mind's conundrums ("Who and where is God?" "Why is there evil?" "Does God answer prayer?") to resolve themselves in orderly fashion.

In such wretched moments, an outcry of prayer—against death, against suffering—is a screaming bond with heaven, stripped free of throat-clearing academic distinctions and subtleties.

As Psalm 61 asserts, when the spirit fades, it's time to pray. Prayer in a time of weakness feels sheepish at first, like a foul-weather friend showing up only when he needs a loan. But the words spring from a molten core of personal truth and plain feeling, before the phrases have time to dress up or soften the blow.

The second verse that jumps out and sinks in is this: "For you, O God, have heard my vows; you have given me the heritage of those who fear your name." Heritage. We can read the Psalms and take them personally, as if they've been airlifted for our use from the land of antiquity, cleaned of historical barnacles and ready to go. They somehow field my confused emotions and hand them back to me as words that work nightly miracles in the dark.

Lead me to the rock
that is higher than I. . . .
Let me abide in your tent forever.

PSALM 62: *Candlepower*

For God alone my soul waits in silence.

The church down the street recently started a Friday night service. I finished work last night in furious haste and ran to the sanctuary to join my wife for the six PM start-up. I teetered into the pew in a zombie state, work-numb, body humming like a tuning fork from the day's phone calls and squeezed-in extra stories to write. Not the best mood for church.

But the service didn't ask my opinion. It went about its business, instantly giving off new messages of its own. Candlelight glowed in every darkened corner. The aisles flowed with dancers. Medieval chant poured down from the balcony. My knotted jaw loosened and dropped. The power of the moment chipped away at my fussy, protective shell. The day's sheen of anxiety evaporated. Ears, eyes, nose, and mouth all became open portals, suddenly unplugged. A couple of breaths later, the body relaxed enough to reveal interior energies, now unburied. A globe of internal light expanded to natural proportion, having waited all day to shine. It had been crammed in a dark place until the day's comically earnest tasks and official processions could pass.

That's how the soul's rising feels to me. The whopping wager of religious tradition is that God instigates such movements. The soul had been waiting in silence all day for the right moment, patiently reserving judgment, trusting I'd open the right door once the sun went down. The soul: God's deputy, an earthly proxy who waits with you and for you to make an opportune moment for the candle to glow.

And when the soul's light does come out of the womb of silence, we realize we're finally catching up to this psalm, its wisdom buried under the blizzard of the day's memos, invoices, and sticky notes.

Pour out your heart before him;
God is a refuge for us.

PSALM 63: *Wallet–Size*

My flesh faints for you,
as in a dry and weary land.

Some psalms seem embedded in their time, wearing long robes from a Hollywood biblical epic or referring to controversies hard to retrieve now. Not Psalm 63. It reads fresh off the page, a declaration of spiritual passion, hunger, and happiness: "My mouth praises you with joyful lips."

This is a psalm for everyone to keep on a little folded-up piece of paper in purse and wallet, the way a journalist keeps a copy of the First Amendment handy—for inspiration, a reminder of first principles to take out during the wait on the subway, in the doctor's office, or before the firing squad: "For you have been my help, and in the shadow of your wings I sing for joy."

Despite all the enforced divisions between faiths—doctrinal, left-wing, right-wing, racial, socioeconomic—Psalm 63 salutes the values that beckoned people to the life of faith in the first place—a taste for transcendence, the dignity of the search, ethical commitment, community.

People who read Psalm 63 from their own respective religious camps might be startled to find common ground after all; the words summon refreshment and spiritual breakthrough. Just about everybody has felt this joy or wants to; surely all share invisible membership in the sentiment of this one psalm, a spiritual friendship, a religious movement across the millennia. They might even wonder what all the fighting was about.

So I will bless you as long as I live;
I will lift up my hands and call on your name.

PSALM 64: *Annoying*

Hide me from the secret plots of the wicked,
   from the scheming of evildoers.

God knows, people are moody. Eruptions and elations come and go like wind gusts, unpredictably. The Bible has its moody moments too. Psalm 64 is one—a frantic complaint about enemies and the fantasy of expectation that God should ambush all the bad guys. You seldom hear this psalm in a worship setting. It goes head-on against the biblical teaching of love your neighbor. It's alarming to find such harping for vengeance in the pages of the word of God: "God will shoot his arrow at them; they will be wounded suddenly." But there it is, Psalm 64 in black and white, all the more curious since it's followed by Psalm 65's embrace of blue skies and high spirits.

Psalm 64 is there for a reason. It's full of raw emotion—the undigested, real feelings of the victim of crime. The hideous things that happen in the real world usually get edited out when formal religion has the floor—bitter experiences, angers, mistakes, dark thoughts, harrowing stories of crime and victimhood, abuse, heartbreak: "For the human heart and mind are deep."

But for the moment the Bible yields time to an annoying, disagreeable, hurting person who ruins the tenor of the sacred assembly with honest discontent. And if I run into such a person at worship this week, will I this time reserve judgment?

Hear my voice, O God, in my complaint;
   preserve my life from the dread enemy.

PSALM 65: *Groundswell*

You visit the earth and water it,
you greatly enrich it;
the river of God is full of water.

My wife and I took a trip out West—the Colorado mountains, Dakota Black Hills, the Great Plains of Nebraska and Wyoming. It was an amazing time of encounters with elk and antelope, as well as a season of fine weather and late summer on the High Plains. We were just passing through—fair-weather friends in a rental car. We didn't have to ponder what it's like to live there in winter when wind chills can dive to forty below. We make poetry of scenes of nature but walk away when things get chilly. Nature carries on either way, with or without us.

"The meadows clothe themselves with flocks, the valleys deck themselves with grain, they shout and sing together for joy." Psalm 65 says nature rejoices at the presence of God the creator. It suggests that nature has its own relationship with God that we're not privy to, and we have no right to resent it or try to break it up. The relationship between God and nature has its own rhythms and vocabulary, giving away few secrets. And it's a lot older than the human relationship with God.

"You make the gateways of the morning and the evening shout for joy," Psalm 65 declares. OK, it's nature's party, not ours. The psalm also praises nature for its willingness to share its gifts with us, a thanksgiving for a successful harvest—"You crown the year with your bounty; your wagon tracks overflow with richness."

This psalm might sound naive and over the top at first—"the hills gird themselves with joy." They do? If so, it looks like nature has its own emotions, integrity, and personality, maintaining continual conversation with the Almighty. Step outside and eavesdrop: The sounds of earth are bearing witness to their creator and ours.

You are the hope of all the ends of the earth
and of the farthest seas.

PSALM 66: *Beethoven*

Make a joyful noise to God, all the earth;
  sing the glory of his name;
  give to him glorious praise.

The history of music and worship and even theology might have turned out differently if the original music of the Psalms, now lost, had survived in all its tuneful glory and technique. The songs, in any case, would inhabit us. Surely we'd learn them around the religious school campfire and whistle them unconsciously at work. They'd be on CD and packaged in every conceivable way, stretched to every pop genre.

Psalm 66 launches itself on cadences and emotions that seem on the verge of bursting out in song: "I cried aloud to him, and he was extolled with my tongue. . . . Blessed be God, because he has not rejected my prayer or removed his steadfast love from me." The psalm delivers gusts of glory, hope of reconciliation, blessing, gratitude.

Soon it will be New Year's, and I'll do what I traditionally do: Put Beethoven's Ninth on the stereo. It's a kind of psalm, a nineteenth-century version. It's like a flare in the sky, a way to turn the page on the new calendar and start afresh, an act of renewing membership in the human race. Beethoven's bigger-than-life music, set to the "Ode to Joy" poetry of Schiller, constitutes a letter to the world, a plea for human camaraderie, a cry as well to the God above for divine acceptance. Despite Beethoven's personal suffering—his deafness, loneliness, bad bowels—his music found a way to lift its listeners to their best selves, swelling with a nobility worthy of divine notice.

The Ninth's theme of divine watchfulness catches some of the spirit of Psalm 66. Both are cries to heaven, and both end in joy.

Come and hear, all you who fear God,
  and I will tell what he has done for me.

PSALM 67: *Farmers, Heroes*

The earth has yielded its increase;
God, our God, has blessed us.

These days, few of us know any farmers or anything about harvest time or the difficulties of farming or the relief a farmer feels after a decent crop despite the odds of weather, insects, and bad prices. Fewer people live on farms now, which means fewer human contacts with the annual fertile drama of earth and sky.

Here in Tennessee, despite the fine rural scenery and soil, the number of dairy, swine, and cotton farms has decreased. The average age of farmers here is nearing sixty, and fewer children are taking up the business. This shift amounts to a crisis in the making, but people are unaware of it; they see grocery stores stocked with fresh produce year-round, increasingly due to imported goods.

In an asphalt world of suburban sprawl and online commerce, we can go for years without thinking about the earth's miraculous yields and edible bounties. We can live a busy illusion of sophistication and independence for a while, but it changes nothing: We're as dependent on the earth as ever.

Psalm 67, a harvest prayer, reminds us of the long story of our reliance on forces greater than ourselves. To renew acquaintance with the story, try fasting as a way to feel that humbling dependence or get to know some farmers and their economic issues. Ask them about Psalm 67's words—"God be merciful unto us, and bless us; and cause his face to shine upon us" (KJV). They might talk as if their lives depended on it.

May God continue to bless us;
let all the ends of the earth revere him.

PSALM 68: *Mishmash*

O rider in the heavens, the ancient heavens;
  listen, he sends out his voice, his mighty voice.

Take your Bible, get comfortable, and open it to Psalm 68. See how long you last. It's considered the most difficult psalm to understand in the whole book. With lengthy heavenly descriptions of military conquest and salvation, it gives fits to scholars who say it's a tossed salad of fragments, chopped up and thrown together from sundry places. The psalm provides fascinating details—"Your solemn processions are seen, O God...the singers in front, the musicians last, between them girls playing tambourines." But the parade of images is puzzling. A devout reading might try to harmonize it all or sermonize from a theme or two and leave the rest politely behind.

Every time a reader sits alone in a room with the biblical text itself, a drama begins, a wrestling with the very words of Holy Writ. The phrase "word of God" still rings with sacred authority. This implies that any and every passage from scripture is an urgent message from heaven. Anxiety can settle in, or impatience and boredom, if you butt heads with an incomprehensible passage or translation. Psalm 68 might serve as a test case.

Even when the Bible looks confusing, a certain reality gets clarified. If this is the word of God, a document glowing somehow from contact with transcendent forces, then reading a psalm is like being an honored guest in the court of the divine. Such a guest feels flattered when the conversation is in his language. When it isn't, the guest feels humbled by the realization of the terms of the visit: The reader is not the proprietor but a visitor with no power or privilege of rank. Best to be grateful for the invite, be observant, take good notes, and put it all in the memoir someday.

Lift up a song to him who rides upon the clouds—
  his name is the LORD.

PSALM 69: *Persecuted*

I am weary with my crying;
my throat is parched.

Three times Psalm 69 is quoted in the Gospels. The psalm, a cry of someone persecuted, came to mind among Jesus' followers.

The New Testament reference reminds us that people heard, remembered, and passed along the Psalms in the real, everyday world. By Jesus' time, the Psalms were part of the landscape, offering new messages to the Jewish followers of the Nazarene's ministry. The resurrected Jesus said in Luke 24 that the Psalms would be fulfilled by his coming.

Jesus' suffering transformed Psalm 69. Jesus' defenders found phrases that applied to their Savior's plight—most famously verse 21: "For my thirst they gave me vinegar to drink," which, when viewed as a prophecy, described Jesus' excruciating condition on the cross.

Centuries later a reader looking for prophecy in a psalm should proceed with care lest it negate the original meaning that countless Jews have heard and contemplated over the span of time. Notice how little of the psalm is actually used for prophecy's sake—three verses here. But that leaves 90 percent of Psalm 69 unused or ignored—treated perhaps like a spent carcass, gutted and tossed away.

Psalm 69 has its own authority, its own story to tell. The psalmist was possibly a disciple of the prophet Jeremiah, facing the ordeal of persecution in his own time. The psalm is full of curses, fear of drowning, aching for a divine touch—an eloquence available to any anguished hearer, whether in twenty-first century B.C.E. or twenty-one centuries later.

Save me, O God,
for the waters have come up to my neck.

PSALM 70: *Waiting for God*

But I am poor and needy;
hasten to me, O God!

In a few short lines, Psalm 70 has a confession to make. The speaker admits he doesn't have the God-feeling, the lively faith, that others do. He implores God to arrive, "O Lord, make haste to help me!"

In four thousand years, the world hasn't changed much. People walk around feeling blessed, while, a few inches away, others feel nothing of this. The way of the Spirit is like a tornado's mysterious path, bouncing around from house to house, skipping one while engulfing the next.

Reading this psalm, the famous Samuel Beckett play comes to mind. *Waiting for Godot*, with its fretting, sighing characters on an empty stage, signaled a new sensibility fifty years ago to people still dazed by world war, numbed by destruction and mass murder. The twentieth century revealed new depths of the abyss. Some blamed God for not stopping the wars and the Holocaust. Others concluded we should face up to our own heinous responsibility for the bloodletting: The violence of the century wasn't an indictment of God but of our own stupidities. The horrors of the new millennium, with flames of extremism and fear, offer no respite.

So we wait, often stoically, rather like characters out of Beckett, or even like a character from a psalm, perhaps for a divine verdict, a summons, an arrival. There's something weary about the waiting. So much has happened, so much that demeans human life and divine justice on earth.

"You are my help and my deliverer," Psalm 70 declares, in spite of everything, in spite of all the baggage we carry from the old century into a nervous new one.

Let those who say, "Aha, Aha!"
turn back because of their shame.

Let all who seek you
rejoice and be glad in you.

PSALM 71: *Boomers*

So even to old age and gray hairs,
 O God, do not forsake me,
until I proclaim your might
 to all the generations to come.

Psalm 71 might be the official theme song of the baby boomers, who will soon be staring gray-haired into oblivion. Increasingly, we aging boomers are taking inventory of what we've brought along so far and what it all means, a big cart full of stuff on the postwar path of prosperity. It includes vigorous, vaporous youthful memories—suburban quiet, church solidities, the Beatles, Stones, and James Brown, Andy Griffith and Mary Tyler Moore, anger in the streets and disco on the dance floor.

God always figured into the inventory too, when we took time for the matter, usually more questions than answers. Now boomers slip into a new phase of life, or it slips upon us—a new seriousness, maybe the first real assessment of a situation that Captain Kangaroo never explained, this one-way ticket to mortality we're holding: "Do not cast me off in the time of old age; do not forsake me when my strength is spent."

The psalm writer, pleading from old age, serves up a warning of prospects to come—isolation, drift, fear, regret. But there's also a redemptive turn: Renewal is possible in the face of physical decay, and the psalmist pledges to sing the faith with future generations in mind.

The psalm's attitude is the opposite of nostalgia. It means being generous toward those who'll come next—a sharing of wealth, wisdom, and witness that concedes that our own obnoxiously celebrated generation will one day pass away. It invites boomers to add a legacy to God's continued drama with earth, something besides greatest-hits collections and SUVs. It's our invitation to get serious.

The boomerless future will happen in any case.

O God, from my youth you have taught me,
 and I still proclaim your wondrous deeds.

PSALM 72: *Signs and Wonders*

May his name endure forever,
his fame continue as long as the sun.

I was heading downtown when I saw Psalm 72 quoted on a church message board outside along a busy city street: BLESSED BE THE LORD, THE GOD OF ISRAEL, WHO ALONE DOES WONDROUS THINGS.

It's a religion writer's compulsion to read these outdoor church signs, the more the better. Even when they're ho-hum, they're never less than interesting. They offer clues to the national spiritual mood. They're evangelistic tools, wares of the religious marketplace.

They're also on the increase, I've noticed. So I made a little study of this overlooked science of signs, identifying seven types: 1) the American work ethic (example: PRAY FOR A GOOD HARVEST, BUT CONTINUE TO HOE); 2) fun with puns (THE BEST VITAMIN FOR A CHRISTIAN IS B-1); 3) modern metaphor (GOD HAS AN 800 NUMBER—PRAYER—IT'S ALWAYS OPEN); 4) short essay (THE COURAGE TO SPEAK MUST BE MATCHED BY THE WISDOM TO LISTEN); 5) philosophy 101 (COINCIDENCE IS GOD'S WAY OF STAYING ANONYMOUS); 6) current events (SATAN IS THE ETERNAL TERRORIST); and 7) strict Bible quote.

This last category is what I saw from Psalm 72. The passage comes at the end of a long prayer for an Israelite king. Commentators identify the quote as a conclusion or doxology that brings Book II of the Psalms to an end.

By one estimate, we're assaulted by seven thousand marketing messages a day—TV ads, e-mail spam, billboards and the rest. Churches with message boards (usually Protestant, sometimes Catholic) hope to burn through the clutter and knock some holiness into us or at least give us something to ponder as we sit stuck in traffic.

As church messages go, Psalm 72 isn't as flashy as, say, DON'T GIVE UP— MOSES WAS ONCE A BASKET CASE or FORBIDDEN FRUIT CREATES MANY JAMS or DUSTY BIBLES LEAD TO DIRTY LIVES. But there it was between the "2 for 1" offer at the burger joint and the "gun day" sign at the pawn shop—a reminder to busy twenty-first century motorists of God's "wondrous things." As product placement, it must have worked. I still remember it.

May his glory fill the whole earth.

BOOK III

TOO TROUBLED
to Speak

PSALM 73: *Gas-Guzzlers*

For they have no pain;
their bodies are sound and sleek.

This psalm reads like it was written last week. The doubt, envy, and bitterness about other people's arrogant prosperity sound all too familiar. The psalm writer looks across the room and grinds his teeth at what he sees. This is a far cry from Psalm 1, which confidently declared that the mean people will be blasted away in due course.

Now, seventy-two psalms later, the argument is more nuanced and complicated. The writer lingers longer over the unfairness of godless prosperings. His outrage slides away only when he ducks into the sanctuary. The walls, the altar, the peacefulness all keep a vigil to eternity, the long future of righteousness.

Centuries of organized religion have helped the world find unexpected dignity and hope by inviting this biblical tranquility and beauty into the heart. A house of worship witnesses to a long history of such invitation: "But for me it is good to be near God; I have made the Lord GOD my refuge, to tell of all your works." In such a room the scoffers' noisy parades shrivel to nothing. Their names, stature, and worldly standing die away. Soon they'll be forgotten entirely, and the fuss over them will look all the more inane. "They are like a dream when one awakes; on awakening you despise their phantoms."

The psalm writer makes his choice. He decides it's better to contemplate the abundance of God than the sweet, sickening fumes of envy.

My flesh and my heart may fail,
but God is the strength of my heart
and my portion forever.

PSALM 74: *Screams and Agony*

O God, why do you cast us off forever?
Why does your anger smoke against
the sheep of your pasture?

There are more than five hundred thousand congregations in America. Some of them invite tearful emotion with sobbing testimonials and ministers who cry at the sins of nation and neighborhood and their own flock. The strategy of most, however, remains dignified restraint. No sudden moves. Emotions get flattened out. Sermons, scripture stories, the reciting of the creeds tend to be monotone. The unspoken message of this emotional monochrome is: God doesn't want a wide range of emotions from us. Don't get mad at the Lord.

Reading Psalm 74 turns that message upside down. Lift the veil and you discover a psalm inundated with desperation. The year is 587 B.C.E. The scene is chaos and cataclysm. The temple of Jerusalem has been attacked, and the shocked believers feel abandoned by the Spirit: "They set your sanctuary on fire.... They smashed all its carved work.... There is no longer any prophet, and there is no one among us who knows how long. How long, O God, is the foe to scoff?"

The psalm writer maintains sanity by recalling in powerful tones God's omnipotence: "You divided the sea by your might; you broke the heads of the dragons in the waters.... Yours is the day, yours also the night." There's a plea to the Almighty to remember his covenant with his "dove," Israel. "Do not deliver the soul of your dove to the wild animals; do not forget the life of your poor forever."

During a long season of peacetime, we used suburban decorum to smother the wild spasms of despair and yearning from religious life. Domestic terrorism put us back in touch with the world's savagery. Psalm 74, as if shouted from the back pew, brings news from the broader world of spiritual danger and desire. Suddenly this psalm is waiting to be heard again.

Have regard for your covenant,
for the dark places of the land are full of the haunts of violence.

PSALM 75: *Nearby*

Your name is near.

The nearness of God: It's the proposition that haunts everything. What does it mean? In our world of wireless technology, subatomic big bangs, and evangelistic healings, this divine nearness might be communicated in a dozen ways:

- God exists between the molecules, outside them, in a measureless ether.
- God exists in the molecules, nearer than near.
- God is near in scripture. Read with reverence and you're in the presence of God.
- God withdraws from the space of our freedom so that our free-will choices have integrity, and we're not overwhelmed.
- God comes to us in times of joy and sorrow, times of honest need.
- God upholds everything, keeps life's vibration humming.
- God micromanages the lives of those who believe.
- God is embodied in the Ten Commandments.
- God is within, in our very souls, a wisdom to be unlocked.
- God is creation itself, the physical world, the great outdoors.
- God is right here, right now, watching and touching but physically inaccessible.
- God is near when God's name is uttered.
- God is described by none of the above, not even close.

The psalm world communicates the notion straightforwardly: God is the major player on the field, the Creator and Sustainer. There is no hope of victory or salvation unless God shows up, and God does. Sometimes God does not. Then the assembly complains or accuses itself of a lack of faith and persistently implores God to return, so that the name may indeed be near again.

For in the hand of the LORD there is a cup
*   with foaming wine, well mixed;*
he will pour a draught from it,
*   and all the wicked of the earth*
*   shall drain it down to the dregs.*

PSALM 76: *Grapes of Wrath*

Who can stand before you
when once your anger is roused?

At some point, the phrase "God is love" eclipsed "the wrath of God" as the message on the marquees of the modern religious market. The sentiment is not entirely convincing. The biblical record points to a more complicated history of divine moods. Think of Job's conversation with the whirlwind or some of Jesus' sayings about coming to bring a sword. Or this psalm about God's terrifying power and might, the sudden divine anger defined as the painful distance between human failing and divine righteousness.

Today a huge chunk of pop culture depends on the commercialization of violence, stylized anger, intimidation. Seeking relief from this contamination, people look to houses of worship for reminders of gentleness and acceptance in the larger scheme of the universe. "God is love" reigns.

A law of psychological compensation is at work. In previous decades or centuries when street life and popular culture weren't so coarse, and social relations assumed everyday courtesies between strangers, messages of anger often came from somewhere else—organized religion. Sermons clanged about a wrathful, judgmental God. Perhaps they served as a wise counterweight to the soft gentilities of daily life, a reminder that real life is a balance of shadow and light.

The situation is reversed today. Anger is the code of the West and the East, whether it's feeding road rage or the ferocious resentments of georeligious conflict. The twentieth century's two world wars released a toxin into the bloodstream of the world. Mainstream religion is there to counteract it all with a vision of love.

The closing verses of the psalm don't leave the reader twisting helplessly in the winds of wrath. They advise: Do something. Take action. Go and make a vow of thanksgiving to the Almighty, wrath or no wrath.

Let all who are around him bring gifts
to the one who is awesome.

PSALM 77: *Columbus Day*

I am so troubled that I cannot speak.

Secretly we believe they had it easy in biblical times: Folks heard God in the thunder, which made it a snap to believe. No existential crisis for them, no all-night, dorm-room arguments about God's existence. But that's a cliché, and Psalm 77 offers something more interesting than the cliché—a climate of human panic and divine absence, despite memories of the rock-solid divine deeds of yesteryear. Where is God now? "Has God forgotten to be gracious? Has he in anger shut up his compassion?" People knew dread in their bones. Their vivid experience of God had a flip side, the fear that God could leave the scene, withhold blessing as punishment. After such intimacy, withdrawal. That was the existential crisis.

It wasn't so different from the spiritual calculus of our day. Pockets of believers claim miracles or divine contact or declare the hand of God is blessing the nation or turn steadily to Bible stories that keep them in touch with God's grandeur. Other people experience an utter spiritual blankness, a search on the sea for signs of shore. Each morning brings the hope that maybe today will be Columbus Day, the day a new spiritual world is discovered.

Ministers see the passions stirred at sports events and wonder why such extravagant emotion isn't caught at the worship hour. Oftentimes congregational worship life falls into its own form of cliché: Everybody leaves after an hour and fifteen minutes; no one departs much from the script; questions go unanswered.

Psalm 77 won't have that. It contains passionate fear, disappointment, hope, all let loose in the communal setting. There's permission to plead the way back to God. Chances are, everybody else in the room is wondering how to get there too.

> *Your way was through the sea,*
> *your path, through the mighty waters;*
> *yet your footprints were unseen. . . .*
> *I will meditate on all your work,*
> *and muse on your mighty deeds.*
> *Your way, O God, is holy.*

PSALM 78: *Miracle Collecting*

He divided the sea and let them pass through it,
and made the waters stand like a heap.

. . . .

Yet they sinned still more against him,
rebelling against the Most High in the desert.

Connoisseurs of supernatural connection fill the world of faith. Some go from one miracle experience to another. I know one minister who discreetly and repeatedly left his church building to attend a revival across town in order to swoon and be healed, time and again. He needed the fix.

Psalm 78 is a lengthy catalog of God's miraculous interventions on Israel's behalf and the people's repeated insurrections and falling away from faith. They witnessed God's historic miracles—the parting of the sea, the bringing of the commandments—and yet as believers they turned out to be hapless disappointments. Their job was to keep the commandments and remember God's mighty deeds. But the miracles seemed to have little effect on them.

Every day people say they could believe if only they received a sign from God, a personal miracle. Yet would that make such a difference? In some cases it does: A life is transformed forever. But others live on the miracle for a while, then want it again. And if the sign doesn't come, they're swamped with guilt or disillusion.

Jesus performed miracles, reluctantly it seems, and was repaid with his disciples' disloyalty. He was more likely to say, "Blessed are those who don't see, yet believe." In our own time, claims of miracles are ambiguous. Scientific rationalism makes it its business to explain away miracles, pronto. As for those feckless disciples of Jesus, it took the Resurrection to capture them: They never needed replenishment after that.

Three miracles are enough for me every day: the survival of the Jews, the existence of the church, the rising of the sun.

We will tell to the coming generation
the glorious deeds of the LORD, and his might,
and the wonders that he has done.

PSALM 79: *Wall-to-Wall*

They have laid Jerusalem in ruins.

E ach psalm lies open like a smooth ancient hill, a potential archeological dig. If you don't dig past the mossy surface of words, you might miss the drama, the layers of emotion beneath. Reading Psalm 79, we can easily gloss over the human misery gushing below the printed words. The psalm pleads for mercy for a Jerusalem in ruins. Yet who can imagine the actual horror behind the statement, "They have laid Jerusalem in ruins"? It evokes mere Sunday school complacencies if we don't look at the appalling blood-and-guts history of the fall of Jerusalem (it happened more than once)—the hacked bodies, the homeless refugees, the crushing sadness, and religious disillusionment. Psalm 79 reports from the scene of catastrophe, perhaps in the sixth century B.C.E.

By 70 C.E., some forty years after Jesus' death and resurrection, the Romans leveled Jerusalem again, turning the city to rubble, including the sacred Temple. The Romans, brutally thorough, somehow didn't obliterate everything. Left standing was an enormous retaining wall of the Temple. More than nineteen hundred years later, it still stands in the heart of Old Jerusalem. It's the Western Wall, the holiest spot in Judaism. The stone edifice survived to become the symbol of past glories and disasters absorbed by the holy city and of yearnings for the future return of God's Temple dwelling place. Even now, Jews read this psalm at the wall on Sabbath evenings.

Calamity and violence continue to visit the old holy city. At such an intersection of earth and heaven, vast spiritual potency and swirling human danger collide. But people journey there every day to touch the pocked dis-colored wall, to kiss it, to leave written prayers in its crevices—just an old wall, holding every memory of revelation, bloodshed, and courage.

Then we your people, the flock of your pasture,
will give thanks to you forever;
from generation to generation we will recount your praise.

PSALM 80: *Anti-Semitic*

Restore us, O Lord God of hosts;
let your face shine, that we may be saved.

Psalm 80 could have been written in the spring of 1945, when the death camps were opened near the end of World War II for all the world to see—the heaps of bodies, the mounds of human ash, the skeletal survivors, the shamefaced Germans. We live in historic times, among Holocaust survivors who witnessed the worst assault on Judaism in its long history. Psalm 80 contains an echo: "They have burned it with fire, they have cut it down. . . . Restore us, O LORD God of hosts."

Anti-Semitism is with us still in all its predictable fury and self-pity. The need of the scapegoater, the impulse to blame another group for self-inflicted misery, always itches to outpace goodness in human history. Psalm 80 reeks of agony, doubt, and hope of divine restoration: "Turn again, O God of hosts; look down from heaven, and see; have regard for this vine, the stock that your right hand planted." A rival vision hypnotizes the haters: nihilism, the fantasy of annihilation, Hitlerian Armageddon, an insane obsession with fiery self-destruction, a glorified self-hatred.

This psalm is soaked in tears of defeat, probably in the wake of the fall of ancient Israel's Northern kingdom. Confusion and fear reign again. Has God's favor disappeared? "O LORD God of hosts, how long will you be angry with your people's prayers?" The history of the Jews is a long story of horrific historical setbacks and miraculous recoveries. The haters have been there all the way. They've had centuries of practice. Entire academic careers are given over to trying to solve the disturbing staying power of anti-Semitism, its bottomless resentments and psychology. No one ever quite gets a handle on it; it's almost as much a mystery as the survival of Judaism itself, a shadow that follows the faith.

More than fifty years have passed since 1945; Holocaust survivors and eyewitnesses are elderly now, passing from the scene. Commemorations intensify. Reading psalms by the light and the darkness of modern history is not for the faint of the heart.

Look down from heaven, and see;
have regard for this vine,
the stock that your right hand planted.

PSALM 81: *Secret Thunder*

"In distress you called, and I rescued you;
I answered you in the secret place of thunder."

In some psalms the people yearn for God: All will be right again if only God will show up. This psalm reverses the drama: God yearns for the people. God's presence is there if they'd watch for it, but they turn away. They don't obey. Human stubbornness blocks the road to communication. People aren't listening. They don't hear God in the "secret place of thunder."

The phrase throws a curveball. Thunder as we know it bursts in from above with little or no warning. But a "secret place of thunder"? Is it somewhere out in the world, some unknown place of reckoning? Or is it somewhere in the interior, stirring out of a corridor of the imagination?

Fanciful imagination is not an easy fit for biblical religion. Traditionally we suspect that imagination leads people astray from biblical truth toward heretical thought. It's seen as a rival to disciplined study of the words of scripture on the page.

But the secret place of thunder invites the reader to wonder, to look up from the text, and to listen. Psalm 81 offers other unusual images for honoring God: Sing a song by blowing "the trumpet at the new moon" or finding God's sustenance in "the finest of the wheat" or in "honey from the rock." Indeed, "open your mouth wide and I will fill it."

God fills the scene when humans give the matter attention. Look up when you finish reading; imagination is what remains when the text finishes its saying.

"I would feed you with the finest of the wheat,
and with honey from the rock I would satisfy you."

PSALM 82: *Ye Gods*

God has taken his place in the divine council;
in the midst of the gods he holds judgment.

I n Psalm 82 God scolds the lesser gods for their lack of ethics and their inferior status under the Most High. It resembles a scene from mythology: a stage crowded with gods and the Almighty overshadowing all. This psalm scene is not usually lifted up in worship settings or in defense of the faith. The gatekeepers seldom acknowledge the existence of polytheistic outbreaks and residues in the Bible. Orthodoxy's disdain for paganism concedes nothing to the argument that the world was (once) animated with rival gods. They fear that such colorful language in a psalm might comfort the enemy. They'd prefer to herd all these other gods off the cliff and into oblivion.

Yet polytheists and pagan earth-worshipers still exist and thrive, and they might be intrigued to find the God of scripture making a case in this psalm against the other gods. God's words include a summary of ethical political ideology: "Give justice to the weak and the orphan," God urges the gods. "Maintain the right of the lowly and the destitute. Rescue the weak and the needy." Then God puts the other deities in their place: "They have neither knowledge nor understanding, they walk around in darkness." Only the one God towers above now.

In Psalm 82, a relatively unknown psalm, God argues for the right behavior of humans and gods alike. Believers will no doubt take note, but only if they're made aware that this short psalm exists in the first place.

Rise up, O God, judge the earth;
for all the nations belong to you!

PSALM 83: *Bloody Shame*

They say, "Come, let us wipe them out as a nation;
let the name of Israel be remembered no more."

Sometimes there's no break between biblical history and modern times. No rest. Psalm 83 pleads to God to stop the enemies who want to destroy ancient Israel. Millennia later the Nazis tried to do just that, as would other modern foes of Jews—a carryover of hostilities of biblical proportion, four thousand years up and down the line. "They conspire with one accord . . . so pursue them with your tempest and terrify them with your hurricane."

This muscle-flexing rhetoric can turn dangerous in no time flat. Every nation uses religious boasting and claims God's favor; those strategies may even define nationhood. In the Mideast this one-upmanship creates a problem on all sides. Each side has its own equivalent texts where God takes its corner. Name-calling and denunciations of enemies, embedded in some psalms like knots in pinewood, drive latter-day peacemakers and negotiators to hopeless sighs. Is there no way to maintain a religion, any religion, without demanding that God side with its adherents and them only?

That despair continues without much relief until verse 16—"Fill their faces with shame, so that they may seek your name, O LORD." Here seems to be an opening for hope. The phrasing turns human: Redemption and peace are possible if all will admit the bloody shame they carry within, the shame of the violence people do in the name of religion. The enemy is not always a foe out there but the heart of darkness within.

At a time when Israelis and Palestinians tear each other apart, readers should comb scripture again for any clue or hope of honorable solution, any seed of courage.

Let them know that you alone,
whose name is the LORD,
are the Most High over all the earth.

PSALM 84: *Strength to Strength*

How lovely is your dwelling place,
O LORD of hosts!

The late Swiss theologian Karl Barth used to say that he thanked God every time he walked past a synagogue. It was an openhearted thing for a Christian theologian to say, and it caught a truth in its simplicity. To walk is to take the trouble to slow down and look. When you walk past a synagogue, you see a dwelling place of God that keeps faith with more than three thousand years of history, Judaism's life span back to Moses and the parting of the sea. A synagogue is the repository of the Hebrew Bible that gave humanity the Ten Commandments, the sabbath, the Psalms, the ethical passion of the prophets, and the heritage of Jesus. A synagogue stands as a monument of survival against hostility and ignorance, an ark of courage and staying power.

Lovely Psalm 84 records a vivid pilgrimage to the house of worship, a scene that embraces chirping birds and happy pilgrims all giving honor: "My soul longs, indeed it faints for the courts of the LORD; my heart and my flesh sing for joy to the living God."

Mosques, churches, temples, and other houses of worship all over town, all over the countryside, bear witness to transcendence, against all odds. When you happen upon one around the curve of a country road, usually a small, white, wooden church, a shy truth reveals itself: Here's a sturdy little building where news of cosmic import is proclaimed faithfully, modestly, despite lapses of imagination and the inertia of centuries. The open doors of the congregation invite strangers to join in the celebration, where voices sing to the hilt and birds roost in the rafters:

For a day in your courts is better
than a thousand elsewhere. . . .
For the LORD God is a sun and shield.

PSALM 85: *Wandering Heart*

Let me hear what God the LORD will speak,
for he will speak peace to his people,
to his faithful, to those who turn to him in their hearts.

"Speak from the heart," people urge. "Listen to your heart." "Do it to your heart's content." In the galaxy of religious yearning, the heart is more than the body's vital pumping organ. It's the living metaphor of hope and feeling, too huge for the world to hold.

And so two vast spirits seek each other—the human heart and the spirit of the Lord God. This goes to the center of the secret narrative of each day. It drives the mystery of life. God and human heart: two forces ever in search of each other; two purities, unbound by gravity. God and heart—two large, mysterious continents; terrain explored in imperfect weather, in predawn darkness.

Both forces inspire poetry, prayer, partisan faith. Psalm 85 summarizes this long human search for divine consummation: "Surely his salvation is at hand for those who fear him, that his glory may dwell in our land." And when it's time to close the sacred text or go home after the worship service, human heart and spirit of God continue the running commentary between them, the pursuit, the hide-and-seek in this earthly place of wayfarers. We all chart out a path on the quest, encouraged now and then by a feeling of warmth that tells us we're getting closer, we're getting warm.

Faithfulness will spring up from the ground,
and righteousness will look down from the sky.

PSALM 86: *Labyrinth*

Teach me your way, O LORD,
that I may walk in your truth;
give me an undivided heart to revere your name.

Poking around in the Smoky Mountains, I stumbled onto a spiritual symbol of the old and the new, the ancient and the modern: a labyrinth, a coiled path designed to aid meditative prayer and relaxation. Labyrinths were popular in medieval times, then fell into neglect, it seems, until the late twentieth century. Now there are about one thousand of them nationwide.

To walk into a labyrinth is to accept a set of ground rules different from the usual stroll, saunter, amble, or hike. Clock time doesn't count. You forget about it for the twenty minutes it takes to walk the labyrinth. The path, a series of semicircles and hairpin turns, leads to an open space in the center, then back out again. Watching your feet and trusting the path give your thoughts permission to wander, slow down, descend or ascend, find a harbor. You're startled to find you're relaxing. Meditation has snuck up on you.

New thoughts arrive. You notice the stones that mark the path. What a fine thing is stone. The material of sacred objects. Ten Commandment tablets, altars, cathedrals, grave markers. Stone: reassuringly solid, permanent, preceding us, outlasting us.

The path itself reassures: Labyrinths have been walked by believers and questers for thousands of years. The labyrinth is a kind of pilgrimage, the walk of faith. Full of strange turns but a proven path coming out right in the end. Words from Psalm 86 flow gently on a labyrinth walk: "Save your servant who trusts in you. . . . Give ear, O LORD, to my prayer. . . . Teach me your way."

The labyrinth won't solve all the world's problems, but it's a human-scale endeavor that requires no Internet access or expert advice. This modest walk might transport you a million miles in a few moments. Walking the labyrinth gives you the earth underfoot, the sky above, and a little bloom of serenity along the way.

For you are great and do wondrous things;
you alone are God.

PSALM 87: *Census*

The Lord records, as he registers the peoples,
"This one was born there."

G od knows the very number of the hairs on our aging heads, so it stands
to reason God would count the heads of the whole world. That's the
gist of Psalm 87: God as the world's census taker, which suddenly expands
the notion of citizenship beyond national borders and political identities.

Occasionally an editorial or poem will urge us to be "world citizens,"
something grander than feverish patriots. The argument never gets very far.
People live in particular places; any broader citizenship looks vague and bland,
too boundaryless to mean anything. But the psalm insists that the people of
the Book should identify with the city of God, which is larger than mere
nationalism. The city of God connects all believers, regardless of language, in
one sweeping vision of ethical citizenship. This is no sentimental political
fantasy. It's what Jews feel across the Diaspora; it's what Muslims feel across
their ethnic diversity; it's what Christians feel about the church universal. It's
the consequence of a belief in the God of the ages, God of the universe,
which believers declare at worship every week.

Psalm 87 says, "On the holy mount stands the city he founded," and the
capital of this territory of believers is Jerusalem. All roads lead there. Even if
you never visit, your connectedness to it is certain. Faith carries privileges of
citizenship: The spiritual geography has been mapped and cataloged by the
ultimate census taker.

Glorious things are spoken of you,
O city of God.

PSALM 88: *Present Darkness*

You have put me in the depths of the Pit,
   in the regions dark and deep.

Psalm 88 causes a jolt because of what it refuses to offer—hope. The psalmist walks with the prospect of death, in darkness, no light round the corner. It feels unrehearsed. Somehow it evaded editorial changes that would lighten its spirit. It's a psalm with no upturn, no happy ending, perhaps the grim circumstance of serious illness. The spirit that inhabited Psalm 23 has disastrously fled here at nearly the two-thirds mark in the collection of psalms.

The words hover near the place of the dead, asking God for rescue. There's no hint that such will come. "I am like those who have no help, like those forsaken among the dead." The book of Ecclesiastes comes to mind, with its similarly discomforting mood. Ecclesiastes advises that there is a season for everything, a time to live, a time to die.

In the shifting moods of the Psalms, here is a time to face mortality, to "live" with death, stare in its direction and take a measure of it, if this be the time. Elsewhere scripture will announce that death does not have the last word—God is the God of the living. But only after Psalm 88 is done. At times grief or a bad patch of life must be lived through, not cut off too soon or trivialized: "Your wrath has swept over me; your dread assaults destroy me."

This psalm will never win a popularity contest, but its wisdom is plain. There are times for sitting with the darkness, calling out from an awful, desperately threadbare corner to the only keeper of salvation that there is.

Do you work wonders for the dead?
   Do the shades rise up to praise you?

. . . .

But I, O Lord, cry out to you;
   in the morning my prayer comes before you.

PSALM 89: *Enigma*

How long, O LORD? Will you hide yourself forever?
How long will your wrath burn like fire?

Psalm 89 wrestles with enigmas. This psalm, spoken by an Israelite king, begins with the familiar piety of singing God's mercies, rehashing the Lord's covenant with David and the kings of Israel. For thirty-seven verses, the holy language lulls the reader in tones of sanctity.

Then the speaker snaps. He accuses God of betraying all God has promised. The probable reason for the king's anguish is military defeat. He can't understand how God could abandon him and his ancestors at this hour. Seldom is scripture tinged with such bitterness: "You have renounced the covenant with your servant," the king tells God. "You have defiled his crown in the dust." The psalm plants unsettling seeds about the mysterious ways of God: "Lord, where is your steadfast love of old, which by your faithfulness you swore to David?"

The emotional turbulence of Psalm 89, written so long ago, has a modern pitch to it. It reminds me of some worship services I've attended—assemblies of the speechless, a scattering of people who look a little stunned, unable to make much sense of the sacred stories or reconcile them to the chaotic days of their own lives. On such days, the Bible seems to be another world entirely, a world in a book, different from this life of the ticking clock.

The king in Psalm 89, nauseated by defeat, screams his disillusion, his inability to bridge the earlier glory days to the days of his own ruin. He goes public with his confusion. Imagine a political or religious leader doing that today. It would be professional suicide. In a media world of hyperscrutiny and incessant news updates, everyone puts on a bland, reassuring public face.

Psalm 89 embodies a voice of the abandoned and confused, a dissent against death, a heartfelt howl unto the gates of heaven—for everyone since.

Remember how short my time is—
for what vanity you have created all mortals!

BOOK IV

Let the
Earth Quake

PSALM 90: *Futurama*

The days of our life are seventy years,
or perhaps eighty, if we are strong.

A century from now, futurists say, people will live to be 150. Organ harvesting and other genetic manipulations will make this longevity possible. This will double Psalm 90's melancholy math regarding the length of this life. The psalm writer reminds us our time on earth is full of labor and sorrow, and it's short too—seventy or eighty years and "even then their span is only toil and trouble; they are soon gone, and we fly away." From that point of view, doubling our life span wouldn't be something to shout about.

Confident as ever, today's science will surely predict doubling even that 150-year pinnacle some day, then double it again. There will be *Time* cover stories on the promise of reaching human immortality itself on earth. A debate will break out: Who will get to be immortal? Who will be eligible for expensive and limited medical resources? What would quality of life mean to a four-hundred-year-old? Could seven-hundred-year-old senior citizens cope with all the changes in a lifetime of many centuries? Would there be twelve-hundred-year wedding anniversaries?

From the heady heights of scientific speculation and sci-fi fantasy, death is the great embarrassment, a vulgarity, the irrational flaw in the design at the center of everything. Psalm 90 accepts death, practically singing an anthem to it. Why must there be death? It's nature's way of getting us out of the way so others can come along and join the party of life for a while. Knowing the inevitability of death brings zest to life. The outrageous fact of death embodies a biblical teaching: Time is finite; only the Creator is forever. Anyway, if we had immortality on earth, what sort of condition would it be—eternal youth? a progressive aging and shriveling? Could people still die accidentally? If so, imagine the fear that would be the world's constant companion. No one would ever take risks or leave the house.

When science's great fantasies collapse in disillusion, Psalm 90 waits at the finish line for all who are ready to face it.

So teach us to count our days,
that we may gain a wise heart.

PSALM 91: *Literally*

For he will command his angels concerning you
to guard you in all your ways.

To believe in the Almighty is to have the protection of armies of angels and deliverance from pestilence, terrors, snares, and destructions. So announces Psalm 91. How should the reader take this? Literally? Symbolically? There's a bumper sticker that reads, "I take the Bible seriously, not literally."

At the moment I'm reading this psalm at the beach. The light is brilliant; the surf is mesmerizing, draining time of its speed and urgency. The furious issues of the day wash out to sea. In such happy emptiness I pick up the Psalms. They read like messages in a bottle from long ago or like ancient mineral deposits well preserved in geologic formation. The question now is, are they like a mere decorative quartz on the shelf, or do they serve as renewable fuel for daily living?

For many people the Bible is an old relic washed ashore on the pleasure beach of the consumer culture. They open it up to find the words clean and dry but with little context for figuring out the meaning. Sitting in my beach chair, I intend to take the words I read as literally as possible: "You will not fear the terror of the night, or the arrow that flies by day."

After this psalm is done, something lingers—a sense of the grandeur of entering into belief in this God. That's a literal feeling, not symbolic, even on the beach, where the endless crashing waves mock human aspirations and point to a literal miracle before me—the creation of sea and stars and salty air to breathe and eyes for reading messages from far beyond the horizon.

I will protect those who know my name.
When they call to me, I will answer them;
I will be with them in trouble,
I will rescue them and honor them.

PSALM 92: *Monks*

It is good to give thanks to the LORD, . . .
to declare your steadfast love in the morning,
and your faithfulness by night.

P raising God morning and night is a project some people will go to considerable trouble to make their own. Take the Catholic Trappist monks of Gethsemani monastery in Kentucky. Every morning and night since the mid-nineteenth century the monks have sung God's praises in church services—that's seven times a day—and offered their prayers through the many moods of the weeks, the seasons, and the years, all these many decades. Every day they're up at three AM to go to chapel on the monastery grounds. They sing a psalm and urgently ask God to continue the divine watch and reign through the dead of night.

On a recent visit I was among some overnight guests who joined the monks for their three AM prayers, groggily reading along from the visitor gallery. I wanted credit for getting up at such an unpromising hour, but the monks paid us no mind at all. They had their hands full already: lobbying at the door of the divine, offering exertions of thanksgiving and vigil before the Creator of the universe, perhaps for us all.

While the rest of the world frolics and frets and tries to get a little sleep through the night, the monks enact a narrative of old truths, reliving cosmic dramas. Well into their seventies, many of these gentlemen look spry and youthful. They work on the monastery farm by day, making fruitcakes and cheese, regularly putting down their tools to assemble for organized prayer no matter what. "For you, O LORD, have made me glad by your work; at the works of your hands I sing for joy."

One night I took a wrong turn down the monks' dimming hallway. Before the guest master could shoo me away, I saw the monks returning to their cells after another spent round of psalms. They walked slowly, carrying their silence like a candle, as if to keep the light of the ancient words of praise burning clean and bright.

In old age they still produce fruit;
they are always green and full of sap,
showing that the LORD is upright;
he is my rock, and there is no unrighteousness in him.

PSALM 93: *Shoreline*

More majestic than the thunders of mighty waters,
more majestic than the waves of the sea,
majestic on high is the LORD!

The beach means siesta and sunburn, bikinis and barbeque. It's also
Exhibit A in the trail of musings about divine existence. Here the
horizon blurs with the sky, leading to thoughts of Genesis and first things.
The sound of the surf bears constant testimony to the first sounds after the
creation of the earth, the first sounds God heard here, which hasn't stopped
since, always beckoning us to ponder the Hidden Designer of its origins.
The blunt elements of green ocean and yellow sunlight appear as still-wet
smudges from that big moment in scripture when God separated water
from sky, earth from heaven. The bright scene overpowers the day's incessant sectarian arguments and squawking CNN sound bites.

You seldom see a major religious denominational office located along
shorelines and sunny coastal cities. Instead they have soberly inland addresses.
Sun-drenched settings and religious solemnity apparently don't mix. Maybe
they should. If religious leaders relocated to the shore, they could make use
of the awesome details of a coastal scene—towering clouds, flash of dolphin
and pelican, eternal sea—to tap out new communiqués to the world. Set up
office space to track the moods of an ocean gale or the brilliant smears of a
seacoast sunset as a measure of God's design on the world: "The LORD is
robed, he is girded with strength. He has established the world; it shall never
be moved; your throne is established from of old; you are from everlasting."

The monitorings might contain more useful theological news than the
usual denouncements of social trends and human depravity.

Your decrees are very sure;
holiness befits your house,
O LORD, forevermore.

PSALM 94: *Vengeance*

O LORD, you God of vengeance,
*   you God of vengeance, shine forth!*

This is not an easy psalm to love: God is called on to crush all sorts of disappointing people—the proud, the wicked, the arrogant, the murderers, the dull. Somehow an angry malcontent got into the building, into the canon. This psalm indulges a fantasy of violence. Perhaps the psalmist has been victimized or has witnessed terrible violence: "They crush your people O LORD, and afflict your heritage. They kill the widow and the stranger, they murder the orphan."

From childhood we're led to believe the Bible inscribes strictly noble thoughts, exaltations, heavenly emotions, with all impurities burned away by belief. Yet Psalm 94 and several other kindred psalms reject any such simple sentimental view. The emotion here goes against a beloved view of what religion must be—an affair of good intentions and blameless inclusive liturgy.

Psalm 94 expands the range of human real-life emotion found in the Bible. If we find it embarrassing or irritating to read Psalm 94, well, so what? Embarrassment means an expectation has not been met—in this case, an expectation that the text will be high-toned and consistent with our beliefs.

For scripture to evoke real emotion—embarrassment seems a legitimate one—in a reader in the third millennium, nearly three thousand years after the fact, is itself a wonder.

They pour out their arrogant words; all the evildoers boast.
They crush your people, O LORD, and afflict your heritage.
They kill the widow and the stranger, they murder the orphan,
and they say, "The LORD does not see;
*   the God of Jacob does not perceive."*

PSALM 95: *Guitar Solo*

O come, let us sing to the LORD;
let us make a joyful noise to the rock of our salvation!

Back in the old days, music was the great unifier come worship time. The stately hymns, immovable as the altar, unassailable as scripture, rallied everybody around.

Today music marks one of the bitter divisions in religious life. It breaks up congregations, fuels generational wars. Watchdog activists in denominational life tirelessly scan the horizon to make sure "The Old Rugged Cross" gets into the new hymnal—or gets left out.

The old versus the new, traditional music versus pop—it's a debate over the proper way to praise God in a new millennium. New congregations spring up with altars adorned by electric guitars, that postwar symbol of the new power of youth to make their own sound. The choice of pop instruments carries a whole theology, announcing a God who is accessible, not magisterially distant, meeting people where they are, blessing them as never before. The goliath Christian music industry keeps feeding the pipeline of emotional anthems, big production numbers, and the new anointing.

This scene depresses the traditionalists. They thought worship was supposed to inspire their best, not merely the best-selling. That meant dignity of worship and decorum. Organists skilled in the old classical music of Europe feel under siege by new generations raised on MTV's fast-action, adolescent thrills.

This conflict won't be resolved overnight. It might take several generations to find out who won, if anyone. Let the musical advice of the Psalms have the last word:

O that today you would listen to his voice!
Do not harden your hearts.

PSALM 96: *Green*

Let the earth rejoice.

According to the environmentally minded, the earth is heating up. Greenhouse gasses are amassing; species are dying; forests are vanishing; fresh water is spoiling; and gasoline consumption is accelerating. A catastrophe is in the works. It will take a massive spiritual and material reorientation to set things right again and give earth a breather.

Ecology activists look to organized religion as a last hope for educating the world about the crisis. But many faith organizations are slow to embrace the environmental cause. They're ambivalent. Some suspect ecology is mostly a platform for New Age ideology or antibusiness liberalism.

One source of ambivalence is the Bible itself. It declares God made the world and said it was good. Scripture also says God gave humanity dominion over it. Some interpret that to mean we have the green light to use the earth's resources without apology or reverence. Psalm 96 itself provides ammo for both sides in the debate over the role of human stewardship on earth.

"Let the heavens be glad, and let the earth rejoice; . . . let the field exult, and everything in it." To an environmentalist, this means the earth has a right to good health. To spoil earth is to desecrate God's creation. "O sing to the LORD a new song" calls us to exert responsible earth stewardship.

On the other hand, "The world is firmly established; it shall never be moved." Antienvironmentalists see this as a guarantee that God will not let human recklessness destroy the earth. The Lord's "coming to judge the earth" means it's not humankind's role to "save" the earth.

The environmentalists say people of faith can make a difference: pray, recycle, study the issue, contact the politicians. They might also join those from the other side and read Psalm 96 together, wait for wisdom, and work it out. Somehow everyone must proceed on the same green planet.

Then shall all the trees of the forest sing for joy
before the LORD.

PSALM 97: *Stones and Bones*

His lightnings light up the world;
the earth sees and trembles.

No one knows where Moses' bones rest. To this day, no one can name the undisputed location of Mount Sinai or the ark of the covenant. These mysteries launched a thousand modern-day romantic quests for ancient relics. The obsessive search ignores a theological principle at the core of the Bible, as commentators have noted: God's command not to turn mere objects into cult worship.

The Hebrews long ago banished the divinities from stone and storm. They discredited the idols, gave them a bad name. The God of monotheism cleared the divine throat and cleared the decks: God meant to rid the world of self-worship when declaring that God alone was God. When the Hebrews lapsed and worshiped the golden calf, God thundered at them. And they got the message.

Psalm 97 reminds the world of God's exalted status: "The heavens proclaim his righteousness; and all the peoples behold his glory. All worshipers of images are put to shame, those who make their boast in worthless idols; all gods bow down before him."

This scripture does not describe God as a luminous stone statue. The writer steps away from offering any divine portrait at all. The psalmist relies instead on a few images of action and energy—flashes of fire and lightning, earth trembling, people rejoicing.

It was a challenge to use language to describe this God at all. The challenge is no different today. The paradox gives everybody fits—no depictions of God allowed, yet the command to tell others the news of God's kingdom and ethical standards.

The wager of faith is that the paradox is worth the effort. The alternative, the worship of idols, doesn't work: It demeans people to worship the created and not the Creator.

The mountains melt like wax before the LORD,
before the Lord of all the earth.

PSALM 98: *Someday*

He will judge the world with righteousness.

When God finally wins out in the end, things will look different, Psalm 98 says. It's the oldest hope of religion: The world will be run differently when God gets final victory. What will it be like?

This psalm offers ideas and clues. For one thing, the world will sound different. When God establishes rule in the end, nature will step forward and be heard from: The very seas will roar their praise of God, the hills will "sing together for joy." People will listen to nature with new sharpness. They'll hear the music of God, and they will join in by taking up trumpet and lyre and horn to sing the news.

It's tempting to add a few speculations about the ultimate reign of God: World peace will break out. The troops will come home. Navies will stay docked. Centuries of carefully nurtured hostility will vanish. People will see no point in it.

Places of worship will be a twenty-four-hour affair. Prayer will be everybody's second nature. People will walk around with incandescent souls, the glow of finally having found what they're looking for.

What will the weather be like? Will there still be a need for cars and fossil fuels? Will there be funerals? sports? (My hunch is baseball and soccer will still be around. Boxing and hockey, not.) People (being people) will still make mistakes, presumably, but all will be forgiven, not avenged. Newspapers won't be filled with crimes and court battles to report, only new psalms: "Make a joyful noise to the LORD, all the earth."

The psalm's point is that everything will tense up its focus to one thing, the undisputed presence of God. Humanity will finally devote its full attention to the matter. Faith will at last be a matter of facts not arguments.

> *Let the floods clap their hands;*
> > *let the hills sing together for joy at the presence of the LORD,*
> > *for he is coming to judge the earth.*

PSALM 99: *Guy Thing*

The Lord is king; let the peoples tremble!
. . . .
Let them praise your great and awesome name.
Holy is he!

A priest I know sent a letter to his congregation telling them to shape up. Behavior during worship was getting a bit lax, fidgety, unfocused, casual. He felt the need to remind his flock (more than a thousand people) to straighten up and fly right in the weekly encounter with holiness—dress well for church, be attentive, keep the chatter down. You're in God's house, he said. God wants our excellence. Be dignified. Value awe.

The startling letter made front-page news. The priest's missive went against the grain. In the decades after World War II, our lives took a casual turn. Awe lost its grip on us. Psalm 99 is a fountainhead of awe, a symphony of seriousness: "Extol the LORD our God," the psalm exclaims, "and worship at his holy mountain, for the LORD our God is holy."

The commercialism of all corners of our lives leaves us with a taste for irony, not awe. Casualness has become a national style. Lusty cursing is the standard now on TV; traffic no longer stops for funeral processions; a profusion of strip malls and billboards make the horizon a chaos. Even things divine cannot escape. New-style ministers disdain stained glass and silent time. They present God to their congregations as an "approachable guy," a chummy deity. Formality and modesty smack of the pretentious, the emotionally remote. But we pay a price for this casual approach. Alertness to excellence can get dulled. Spiritual exhaustion, a hard-to-name sadness, drapes over the land.

In Psalm 99 God is not a guy. God is ruler of the universe, associated with pillars of smoke, winged creatures, and fearful holiness. God causes the earth to shake.

The undaunted letter-writing priest stuck to his guns. He might yet start a revolution. Last time I checked, he still had his job.

Let them praise your great and awesome name. . . .
let the earth quake!

PSALM 100: *Monkey Trial*

Know that the LORD is God.
It is he that made us, and we are his.

Charming, old Rhea County Courthouse in Dayton, Tennessee, seems an unlikely monument to the twentieth century's most famous debate about ultimate truth. Yet in 1925, it was the scene of the trial of the century, the Scopes "Monkey" Trial. The world gazed upon Dayton and a fearsome showdown on the subject of human origins and biblical truth.

Nearly eighty years later the courthouse still functions. Reminders of the historic to-do echo each July, when local denizens reenact the Scopes Trial and celebrate those dizzying days that made the town famous.

The trial pitted the biblical story of creation against scientific evolution, the book of Genesis against the books of Darwin. Media promoted the trial as a war of fundamentalism versus rationalism, the countryside versus city life, theology versus geology. It was remembered for its wilting heat and occasional face-offs on the nature of truth. In the end evolution won the day in the popular mind with the assertion that the future belongs to science, not religious dogma. Traditional religion retreated in humiliation for a generation or more. But in the early twenty-first century, prickly debate about the merits of Darwinism erupts once more in school boards from New England to the West Coast.

Psalm 100 tersely declares its own divine allegiances on the subject: "It is he that made us." It speaks in generalities, an annoyance both to creationists and evolutionists. But it leaves an opening for a third way, the view quietly held by millions of mainline believers: God sponsors all truth, so the legitimate discoveries of science cannot contradict religious truth.

While an endless debate keeps churning hot air, the patient eloquence of Psalm 100 bides its time:

For the Lord is good;
his steadfast love endures forever,
and his faithfulness to all generations.

PSALM 101: *Leadership Crisis*

I will study the way that is blameless.
When shall I attain it?

In the world of the Psalms, a king's job was straightforward. Psalm 101 offers a checklist of pledges proclaimed by kings at their coronation. It's a leadership list: The king will promote mercy and justice; behave wisely; pursue purity of heart; cut off the wicked, the haughty, the slanderers, and the deceivers; and be mindful of the "faithful in the land." It's hard to know how successful these pledges were. No media commentaries survive.

We citizens today claim to worry about leadership, the lack of it in politics, commerce, and morals. It's easy to be nostalgic about the high-toned political standards of ancient Israel's day. But would modern voters really want that? The last United States president to pursue purity of heart was declared too boring and unpresidential to be reelected. The media culture demands charisma from national leaders The on-camera pressure to be entertaining yet "presidential" tempts politicians to become actors, relying on platitudes and half-truths and avoiding risky revelations from the heart.

To follow Psalm 101 to the letter would lead to political suicide in any conventional sense: "I will sing of loyalty and of justice." "I will look with favor on the faithful in the land." What would it mean to sing of justice? A president who prefers to hang out at the soup kitchen instead of the Federal Reserve would be impeached. Denouncing the prideful ("A haughty look and an arrogant heart I will not tolerate") might mean saying no to the big donors and lobbyists at election time. And being mindful of "the faithful in the land"—would that mean new White House access for Kansas wheat farmers and Pennsylvania Amish?

Psalm 101 advises us to be careful what we pray for. Leadership that upholds biblical values would be a wild ride in a modern democracy, a shock to the system. Verse 7 offers a plausible start as an inaugural day pledge:

No one who practices deceit
shall remain in my house;
no one who utters lies
shall continue in my presence.

PSALM 102: *Withering Grass*

My days are like an evening shadow;
  I wither away like grass.

Not far from town, on a winding country road, there's a small cemetery, the resting place of rural families who lived a century ago.
Behind it runs a narrow river, the Harpeth. And behind that is a large field
with a big flat-top mound in the middle. It's surrounded by a half dozen,
smaller mounds. These mounds are all that remain of a Native American
city of a thousand years ago, a civilization that preceded Columbus by centuries. The big mound in the middle, twenty-five feet high, served as a
foundation for a huge temple, the religious and political center of this
Indian city of perhaps ten thousand people. All gone now, wiped out by
some plague of time—disease, famine, attack by other native peoples, no
one knows. It's now a backdrop to a pleasant ride in the countryside—and a
rebuke to anyone who would deny its lessons of mortality.

Psalm 102 is one of the penitential psalms (the others are 6; 32; 38; 51;
130; and 143), unusually intense cries to God from someone desperately ill
or spiritually ill at ease—the grim music of the impermanence of human
endeavor. The old headstones of the graveyard go back to 1850, which was
a good while ago but nothing compared to the lost tribal mounds a quarter
mile in the distance: "They will perish, but you endure; they will all wear out
like a garment."

Around the bend on the winding country road, a new subdivision goes
up, a shiny complex of impressive houses. One day they will offer their own
ruins as a fitting foreground to this accumulating picture of what passes away,
leaving nothing but the shimmering grass to enjoy its brief day in the summer sun.

Let this be recorded for a generation to come,
  so that a people yet unborn may praise the LORD.

PSALM 103: *Mercy*

The LORD is merciful and gracious,
slow to anger and abounding in steadfast love.
He will not always accuse,
nor will he keep his anger forever.

The news here is so good that Jewish congregations hear it on the holiest day of the year, Yom Kippur. "The mercy of the LORD is from everlasting to everlasting upon them that fear him" (KJV). Some Christian traditions make this passage part of the daily service. It is data to wake up to, information for greeting the morning: "As far as the east is from the west, so far he removes our transgressions from us."

Yet in the slow drip of religion's influence on society, this message doesn't make a big splash. Lots of worshipers feel out of reach of God's mercy because of awful things they've done. They're wracked with anxiety, with no confidence in the concept of forgiveness or making amends. Some attack their dread with compulsive spiritual alcoholism—excessive church committee work or a serial embrace of one world religion after another—in hopes of earning salvation.

But Psalm 103 sends out its waves in every verse, proclaiming the broad reach of God's mercy, mercy inspired by God's compassion for humanity's fragile condition: "For he knows how we were made; he remembers that we are dust."

Mercy becomes the doorway to eternity for those who keep the divine commandments. Though human life is a paltry thing, it still has a place "from everlasting to everlasting" in some divine realm by the sheer endeavor of God's memory of us. God's mercy is where we arrive, a shoreline of ultimate rescue.

The LORD has established his throne in the heavens,
and his kingdom rules over all.

PSALM 104: *Gladden the Heart*

When you send forth your spirit, they are created;
and you renew the face of the ground.

There seems to be a psalm for every mood. Feeling depressed? Try 27 or 103. Happy? Proceed to 97. Need courage? Look at 31. Here at the 104 mark is a psalm for the bighearted, contented feeling of walking around the block and observing trees, birds, and sunset, your place in the work-in-progress painting called nature.

This psalm retells the Genesis story of Creation. It follows the outline of God's original actions—first God created light, followed by sky, earth, animals, people. Everything enjoys God's attention. Not one breath is taken without God's sponsorship. No lion roars except to acknowledge God's glory. The ships on the horizon, the sun's rising: "When you send forth your spirit, they are created; and you renew the face of the ground."

This psalm even endorses the drinking of wine. This startling detail contradicts the torrent of religious shame that is poured on any who dare commit the sin of enjoying a glass of wine or beer with a meal. Here in the bright light of Psalm 104, wine is brought forth to "gladden the human heart." Reproach, stigma, and dirty looks fall away. The official party poopers are officially drowned out.

Psalm 104's lengthy homage to good feeling furrows its brow only at the end, nodding to the destruction of sinners: "Let sinners be consumed from the earth, and let the wicked be no more."

Sketching the works of God on such a huge canvas, the psalm writer adds his signature in the corner, his two cents' worth, words outlasting him and now preserved as part of Holy Writ itself:

I will sing to the LORD as long as I live;
I will sing praise to my God while I have being.

PSALM 105: *Covenants*

O offspring of his servant Abraham,
children of Jacob, his chosen ones.

Whenever a Christian celebrity casually lets slip that Jews should convert to Jesus, it makes national news either as a reckless romp of religious insensitivity or an act of courage. Whenever a Protestant church renews its efforts to evangelize Jews, it gets Americans talking about unresolved matters of truth and ethnicity.

Such headlines strike a nerve and divide people. One side applauds the action for breaking with political correctness and publicly saying what many others believe—that Jews should indeed come to Christ. The other side thinks it's inconsiderate and morally obtuse to focus yet again on Jewish salvation; because of the Holocaust, Christians have disqualified themselves from presuming to speak for the spiritual welfare of Jews.

Psalm 105 weighs in to reaffirm the integrity of God's covenant or special relationship with the Jewish people: "He is mindful of his covenant forever, of the word that he commanded, for a thousand generations, the covenant that he made with Abraham."

Recently a group of local Christian ministers visited the Holocaust museum in Washington, D.C., at the invitation of a local rabbi. The experience pierced the Christian clergy deeply. The museum's presentation of Western anti-Semitism and Jewish suffering left them shaken and tearful. They came home resolved to promote friendship with Jews and respect for the Jewish covenant with God. Most of them now embrace a Christian interpretation that steadily gains ground: Jesus Christ extended the covenant of God to the Gentiles; the Jews' covenant with God remains intact with its own integrity.

This tension over the Christian instinct to evangelize Jews will never be resolved this side of the kingdom of God. But the Christian ministers' group discovered, or rediscovered, an overwhelming truth—it's one Bible, one ancestor Abraham, one God that everyone shares.

For he remembered his holy promise,
and Abraham, his servant.

PSALM 106: *Mistakes Were Made*

But they soon forgot his works;
they did not wait for his counsel.

This psalm is revolutionary. Its words fly against every modern rule and instinct of public relations in organizational life. The modern rule says put the best publicity face on the matter. Deny, evade, or obstruct for the greater good of reputation and the reassurance of the stockholders.

Psalm 106 dares to go its own way, frankly admitting the religious lapses and mistakes of ancient Israel against God. The psalm's admission of sin is chiseled into the very heart of scripture. This public airing of dirty religious laundry was always part of the basic identity of Israel's life with God. There's no whitewash, no press release sanitized by the lawyers: "Both we and our ancestors have sinned; we have committed iniquity, have done wickedly. Our ancestors, when they were in Egypt, did not consider your wonderful works; they did not remember the abundance of your steadfast love."

Mistakes were made. Ever since, organized religion can't always make up its mind about its own public stance of contrition. It's not sure whether to show itself to the world as the picture of saintly perfection, God's unsullied citadel on earth—or as a hospital for the spiritually wounded, a place of honest emotional vulnerability, laced with a sense of humor. Both styles of congregational life are plentiful. They send mixed signals to the world about what authentic religion really looks like.

Biblical religion gives people permission to own up to mistakes and transgressions. God demands perfect righteousness but also offers mercy to resoundingly imperfect humanity. That paradox is where life gets lived and the drama of redemption unfolds. See Psalm 106 for details.

Nevertheless he regarded their distress
when he heard their cry.

. . . .

Happy are those who observe justice,
who do righteousness at all times.

BOOK V

SPIRIT
Rising

PSALM 107: *Rumors and Roses*

Then they cried to the LORD in their trouble,
and he delivered them from their distress.

P salm 107 swarms with people in all their diverse conditions of misery
and thanksgiving. It recounts sweltering travels and travails of believers—the yearnings, missteps, epiphanies—and the stirrings of God to deliver
them to a vision of love.

A few years ago in the heat of July I watched forty thousand people converge in the Georgia countryside outside Atlanta—a sea of pilgrims expecting a miracle. The occasion was the announcement of the latest message from
the Virgin Mary, declared by a middle-aged woman who claimed to enjoy
regular apparitions of the mother of God.

The Catholic tradition of Marian visions is an old one. Visionaries consistently state that Mary's message urges the world to pray for peace and to
convert one's heart to the gospel. Another tradition usually attends the
apparition scene—that of paranormal or miraculous assertions by pilgrims.
Individuals claim seeing the sun dance or rosaries turning gold or notice the
sudden smell of roses, roses being a favored symbol for Mary.

I'd heard of such strange signs and graces for years. At the Georgia site
that afternoon, it was uncomfortably warm; but everyone waited quietly.
Public-address speakers announced the woman would offer Mary's message
in ten minutes. While I wandered about, looking for locals to interview, I first
noticed it—the faint smell of roses. Perhaps the slight breeze was carrying
perfume on the wind. As I walked, the fragrance persisted. I did not ask anyone else about it. Either they smelled it too, or they didn't.

What did it mean? Maybe it could be explained naturalistically. Yet I felt
no urge to dissect the circumstances or produce well-rounded explanations:
This was not a seminar. Its timing and persistence were intriguing. I took it
as a moment for gratitude—nothing more, nothing less. Wind and earth provide transports of transcendence. A few minutes later the scent vanished. But
not my wonder.

Let them thank the LORD for his steadfast love,
for his wonderful works to humankind.

PSALM 108: *Hot Spot*

"Moab is my washbasin;
on Edom I hurl my shoe."

Touring Israel with a group of American journalists some time ago, we went everywhere—Tel Aviv, West Bank, Golan Heights, Masada, Dead Sea, Jerusalem. One lasting impression: Israel and its famous places are preposterously small. Israel is hardly bigger than New Jersey. Jesus' places of death, burial, and resurrection are close enough to be located under one church roof. The original city of David looks to be about six city blocks. Tel Aviv and Jerusalem, emotionally worlds apart, are separated by less than an hour's drive.

The magnificent place-names of the Bible loom bigger in the imagination than on the map. Psalm 108 glorifies God by tallying the places that fail to measure up to God and the holy city—Edom, Moab, Philistia. Geographically these places would be dwarfed by today's metropolitan standards. But the bigger-than-life piety and defiance of their people put them on the map of world religions.

What Israel lacks in square mileage it compensates for by sheer pressure of spirituality per square foot—the bottomless antiquity and hostilities, the beauty of the khaki-colored hills, the conjuring power of names like Shiloh, Nineveh, Golgotha, Hebron, Transjordan, Cana, the Galilee. It's fitting that the Dead Sea itself, gorgeously blue and still, boasts the densest salt content of any body of water in the world. If you wade in and lie on your back, you don't sink. Instead you're thrust to the surface as you float.

At every turn, whether on water or land, the visitor is greeted by fierce embodiments, religious densities: "God hath spoken in his holiness" (KJV). The place is religiously hot to the touch. There's way too much fighting over turf already. Small as it is, the little parcel called the Holy Land is almost more than the earth can handle.

Awake, O harp and lyre!
I will awake the dawn.
I will give thanks to you, O LORD, among the peoples,
and I will sing praises to you among the nations.

PSALM 109: *Curses*

He loved to curse; let curses come on him.

As Mark Twain noted, few things are more satisfying than a well-timed, well-placed curse word or two. Of course, these days cursing is overdone. It loses its impact and flavor. It's been taken over by corporate sponsorship: TV, movies, and music would collapse if they could not flaunt profanity and cash in on the naughtiness. Movie dialogue tries to pass off cursing as edgy entertainment when it usually indicates lazy writing, a tin ear, an empty sneer. It's called "adult language," but it's mostly adults reliving an adolescent thrill by touching the forbidden fruit of blue language.

Cursing in the ancient world wasn't confined to a sophomoric outbursts of dirty words. Cursing had a serious job to do. Human curses were intended to have magic-like powers that do harm to others—with divine help. The curser deployed his colorful, well-crafted curse as a matter of swift justice and retribution. Psalm 109 is engulfed in florid curses:

- "May his children be orphans, and his wife a widow."
- "May the creditor seize all that he has; may strangers plunder the fruits of his toil."
- "May his posterity be cut off; may his name be blotted out in the second generation."

Some English translations confuse us as to who's doing the cursing—the psalm writer or his godless enemy. Later translations take the onus off the psalmist and say the enemy is doing the trash talk. Then the psalm writer strikes back with a countercurse to undo the first one.

By the end of Psalm 109 the psalmist regains perspective: Better to praise God than be consumed by anger. His enemies are silenced by a quality long abandoned by the current gatekeepers of pop culture, a sense of shame.

Let them curse, but you will bless.
   Let my assailants be put to shame; may your servant be glad.

PSALM 110: *Battered*

The LORD is at your right hand;
he will shatter kings on the day of his wrath.
He will execute judgment among the nations,
filling them with corpses.

It's possible to read most psalms straight through, cold, without much stumbling, without an armful of books and commentaries. Their accessibility is key to the Psalms' popularity. Relatively few historical references trip up the reader or force a call to the experts.

But the Psalms are not airtight vessels that get no exposure to the wind and weather of politics and history. Psalm 110 has extra grit in its teeth, reading like it's right out of a clay canister and giving off the musty smell of a scroll that survived the blinding sand from long, long ago.

It's a short psalm of beautifully obscure verses: "From the womb of the morning, like dew, your youth will come to you." We see moments of clarity—God deputized the Israelite king to carry out the divine mandate and face his enemies. But scholars say the surviving text of this psalm is hard to figure out; perhaps the corroding dust of history damaged the parchment.

Nevertheless, the psalm probably formed part of a liturgy for the coronation of a king. The New Testament writers accorded this psalm great authority. Quoting from Psalm 110, they saw it as a prophecy of the coming of the Messiah, the coming of the day when the enemies of Jesus would submit to his lordship: "The LORD says to my lord, 'Sit at my right hand until I make your enemies your footstool.'"

Denizens of literalism do not regularly cite Psalm 110. Literalism suggests the biblical text is clear, easily understood, and easy to follow. Psalm 110's musty patches remind us that it springs not from Sunday school class but from the frightening lengths of literal time with ancient echoes from a battered earth, the place God chooses to reveal the divine story.

He will drink from the stream by the path;
therefore he will lift up his head.

PSALM 111: *Shock and Awe*

The fear of the LORD is the beginning of wisdom.

This verse, one of the most famous in the Bible, is hard to hear afresh. "Fear of the Lord" is a phrase crusted over with browbeating associations from those scary fire-and-brimstone sermons of yesteryear (or yesterday, depending on the church).

But fear of the Lord, it seems to me, is more akin to feelings of awe than scariness. Awe commands deepest reverence. It takes the breath away. It carries also a flash of terror—hence the fear factor. A feeling of fearful awe is a sure sign you're in the vicinity of holiness. Silence is advised. In the presence of holiness, it's a good idea to remove the hat and shut up. In these days of "shock and awe" military campaigns, religious awe gets confused with the humanmade sort. We forget the distinction at our own peril.

And so it says: "Fear of the LORD is the beginning of wisdom." Yet "wisdom" has a difficult ring to it nowadays too. It sounds dignified, remote, intimidating, chiseled in marble, a subject for saints and spiritual experts, not the daily grind.

But no. Wisdom, in the Bible, means coping with real life. It's practical, sensible, based on human experience. It preoccupies itself with right action, right choices within reach, right relationship between God and earth. It looks around and asks questions about injustice, hypocrisy, even traditional ways of faith, all in the name of finding out the proper way of living honestly day to day in God's creation.

Entire sections of the Bible are given over to Wisdom literature—Job, Proverbs, Ecclesiastes. It isn't heavily threaded with stories of Israel's sacred history or God's mighty acts. It's geared to something more modest—the business of living, contentment, adult responsibility on God's earth. Psalm 111 sings of wisdom themes. It offers advice: Praise the Lord; study the works of the Almighty. Remember God's mercy and redemption. Fear God, feel the holiness. Let your life flow from awe. Let the wisdom begin.

He sent redemption to his people;
*   he has commanded his covenant forever.*
*   Holy and awesome is his name.*

PSALM 112: *Without Fear*

The wicked see it and are angry;
*   they gnash their teeth and melt away;*
*   the desire of the wicked comes to nothing.*

I n a time of lurking fear, runaway heartless wealth, and cynical politics, Psalm 112 reads like a tonic, a reminder that life's conduct in God's world is finally a simple matter: "They rise in the darkness as a light for the upright; they are gracious, merciful, and righteous. It is well with those who deal generously and lend, who conduct their affairs with justice." Fear doesn't get the last word: "They are not afraid of evil tidings; their hearts are firm, secure in the LORD."

Evil is alive and well, a deadly business and no joke. But there's also something ridiculous about it. The cartoon caricatures of dastardly bad guys preserve a truth—their unsuitability as crooks, their inability to enjoy their ill-gotten gain. They do terrible deeds for money or power or media attention. Then what do they do with the spoils? They sit around bored in the big house, too mean to have friends, too paranoid to govern. Suspicion eats them alive. All they know to do is plot more mischief. Every messed-up leader, secular or religious, imposes his or her personal miseries and self-pity on the rest of us and conveniently calls it God's will.

Psalm 112 ridicules the self-absorption of evildoers: They choose to be cruel; they don't respect the Almighty. It doesn't have to be that way. People can choose to join a fearless new world of divine love and trust.

One theory of divine creation says God made the world and populated it as a solution to divine loneliness. People have the freedom to embrace the relationship, the unfolding story of the universe.

The history of faith is built on such choices every hour of the day.

Their hearts are steady, they will not be afraid;
*   in the end they will look in triumph on their foes.*
They have distributed freely, they have given to the poor. . . .
*   They will be remembered forever.*

PSALM 113: *War on Poverty*

He raises the poor from the dust,
and lifts the needy from the ash heap,
to make them sit with princes,
with the princes of his people.

In daily journalism you interview poor people from time to time. The encounters can be uncomfortable at first. Some are homeless people seriously ill, mentally tormented, or just feeling lousy. Or they're angry at the media for neglecting their plight. Sometimes they have long, outrageous tales to tell of government conspiracies and corporate rip-offs whose details might or might not be true.

Sometimes these encounters with the poor are conciliatory. Aware that their ragged situation or appearance makes you a little nervous, they try to ease the discomfort with their own charm or cordiality; for once, they can do something for somebody else, which breaks the long chain of condescension they meet with every day. In the course of a night's stay at the local shelter, they'll tell you colossal stories of adventure, goals for the future, warm memories of home.

Psalm 113 delivers startling news. After proclaiming effusive blessings of God, the psalm identifies the Lord's traits and lists only two: care for women who can't have children and care for poor people.

Our society doesn't make sense of the poor, who don't fit in the scheme of capitalist salvation. We blame poor people for not improving their situation. We dismiss the poor—or romanticize them for their innocence. Neither tendency requires actually meeting any of them. Yet suburban, affluent people who reach out to homeless people in soup kitchens and shelters always find the experience enriching, receiving far more than they give.

In the divine economy, society's poor—irascible, fatigued, or coughing badly—disperse gifts that will never be advertised or given a value in a retail world that stays busily out of earshot of Psalm 113.

Blessed be the name of the LORD
from this time on and forevermore.
From the rising of the sun to its setting
the name of the LORD is to be praised.

PSALM 114: *Everybody's Exodus*

The sea looked and fled.

When the sea parted and the Israelites escaped out of Egypt, the world was turned inside out. God's miracles became part of history's story. In less than two dozen lines, Psalm 114 boils down the biggest event in Hebrew scripture to a few deft images: "The sea saw it, and fled: Jordan was driven back. The mountains skipped like rams, and the little hills like lambs" (KJV).

Outsiders call it a fiction, mere poetry. Believers have other ideas. We hear the Exodus story and its images at worship and quietly translate them in our own way. We bring our own navigational skills to the Bible's story, our own way of making sense of it. With time, the images come to inhabit a believer's own interior landscape.

This operation, this unspoken work of interpretation, happens every time a person goes to worship or opens a Bible. It almost always goes unsaid. And what would we say? That the miracle of the Exodus is true? untrue? Flatly declaring one or the other won't persuade the people next door to agree or disagree. They must ask themselves their own questions: What does it mean that the Exodus story is true? How do I understand that the Exodus really happened with God's help?

Belief is an imaginative act. No matter how many believe the Exodus story, no one will describe the how, what, or why of it in exactly the same way. Each believer's faith is mysterious and snowflakelike, never identical. Each imagination is unique, the internal combustion of religious belief. It generates heat and movement. What remains long after is conviction.

"Tremble, O earth, at the presence of the LORD," verse 7 says. We might interpret this line or explain it away in a hundred ways. But each person who believes it feels a tremor in the bones.

> When Israel went out from Egypt,
>   the house of Jacob from a people of strange language,
> Judah became God's sanctuary,
>   Israel his dominion.

PSALM 115: *God-fearers*

He will bless those who fear the LORD,
  both small and great.

I keep waiting for the God-fearers to make a comeback. In ancient times the God-fearers were Gentile converts to Jewish monotheism who didn't adopt Jewish dietary laws or circumcision. They embraced a few strong biblical principles of life and faith and made a religion of it. They rate a mention in Psalm 115, a poem that ridicules the paltriness of handmade idols and gods.

The God-fearers show up elsewhere in both Testaments, always on the margins. It suits them. Theirs isn't a flashy faith—there's not much ritual or liturgy—but it has the merit of being simple, humble, uncluttered. They're not the chosen people, but apparently they were confident in their salvation, confident they were pleasing God by keeping God's commandments.

A modern-day version might be a group called the Noahites. I've met some in the rural South, a cadre of former Christians who found their way back to an older faith by reading and meditating on the Old Testament. This group was a Protestant church before the members slowly stripped themselves of Christian doctrine, namely the Trinity. First they took down the steeple. Then they abandoned Christmas. Finally they jettisoned Easter. They went back to the covenant God made with Noah (seven commandments gleaned from Genesis—including no idolatry or adultery, no theft or murder, no taking God's name in vain) and appended themselves to that.

In the Bible belt, this was a courageous pilgrimage. Perhaps their simplicity will find appeal in the broader climate of restless spiritual questing. It's had its day before. It may yet have another. The rest of us are left to ponder the words of Psalm 115:

Not to us, O LORD, not to us, but to your name give glory,
  for the sake of your steadfast love and your faithfulness.
. . . .
You who fear the LORD, trust in the LORD!
  He is their help and their shield.

PSALM 116: *Heal*

Then I called on the name of the LORD:
   "O LORD, I pray, save my life!"

I've covered five or six faith-healing events—huge arena gatherings where thousands of people focus on the stage moves of the shouting, praying person at the microphone. These events follow the same formula and invite the same response from the participants who line up on stage, waiting to be healed of maladies one by one.

The healer leans forward to ask what miracle of healing the sufferer needs, then stretches out a hand, declares a prayer, and touches the person with a flourish in Jesus' name. The sufferer might then swoon, collapsing to the floor, as if to get a few minutes' rest from the burdens of this life. Gentle, able-bodied associates catch the person as he or she falls.

In Psalm 116 the writer offers deep thanks to God for overcoming personal, debilitating illness. An unusual tone comes through, the tone of an individual praying quietly in a room. The voices in other psalms often project from a podium, a public rhetoric more suited to congregational speech. This psalm expresses the words and feelings of a lone individual—anguished at first, then grateful and relieved: "For you have delivered my soul from death, my eyes from tears, my feet from stumbling. I walk before the LORD in the land of the living."

A faith-healing service fills an arena with yearning and drama. Depending on your point of view, it swirls with miracles—or wishful thinking and peer pressure. The focus stays on the healer. We don't hear much from the persons healed. Psalm 116 gives voice to the grateful individual thanking the Creator, whether the well-lit stage of the celebrity faith healer comes to town or not.

Return, O my soul, to your rest,
   for the LORD has dealt bountifully with you.

PSALM 117: *Shorty*

Extol him, all you peoples!

Here's the shortest psalm in the book. The New Revised Standard Version packs it into seven lines. Then it stops. The words don't look particularly remarkable at first. It seems odd that the Bible-shapers would bother to shoehorn this one in at all. But slowly the psalm reveals its sense and power. Here it is in full: "Praise the LORD, all you nations! Extol him, all you peoples! For great is his steadfast love toward us, and the faithfulness of the LORD endures forever. Praise the LORD!"

The brevity allows focus on every word. The psalm arrives like a telegram, a break in the action, a brief interruption, a summary of the flow of longer psalms before and after. It's a communiqué of first principles, which might be summarized as

- Praise God, everybody.
- The Lord's merciful.
- The Lord's forever.
- Praise God.

Psalm 117 functions as a foundation stone for the spiritual realm. God's mercy and God's everlasting truth burn as twin flames, illuminating the character of the creator God. The human capacity to express praise of divine life and to imagine everlasting truth is a sign of that mercy and a gift from God. An unbroken stream of believers, some four thousand years running, embodies the conviction of this shortest of psalms.

> *For great is his steadfast love toward us,*
>   *and the faithfulness of the Lord endures forever.*

PSALM 118: *Mere Mortals*

It is better to take refuge in the LORD
*   than to put confidence in mortals.*

My wife and I attend a church that offers Communion at every service, which means less time for the sermon. It's a wise and ancient arrangement.

By contrast, when a worship style calls for a forty-minute sermon, then the minister is center stage and dominates the proceedings. It's about performance, appearance. Many such preachers are tempted to think they're the most important personality in the room, and we are tempted to think so too. By placing huge hopes on the power of a really long sermon, we anoint the pulpiteers in inappropriate ways. They become the franchise. The rhythm of their speech and the very will of God get blurred into one blinding fog machine of rhetoric.

Then one day the minister messes up, proving he or she is human after all. We're shocked that it happens—the moral lapse, the abuse of power. We forget that the power we gave to the position created the conditions for the fall—unusual access to people's private lives or the church's money or the presumption to talk for God. Authority can slide into authoritarianism.

Better to spread the religious authority around at worship time: locate it in the bread and wine; in the music; in the lay leadership, as well as the sermon. Don't concentrate all of it in one personality in a pulpit. It's not fair to the minister.

Psalm 118 talks about finding salvation by God's power, not people's promises: "I thank you that you have answered me and have become my salvation. . . . This is the day that the LORD has made." People today worry that a hundred trends of popular culture undercut leadership: the speed of change, the dominance of pollsters, the attention deficit of consumers, the tyranny of hipness that sneers at the past.

People of faith need leaders. Paradoxically, the best leaders inspire confidence even as they quote from Psalm 118:

> *Open to me the gates of righteousness,*
> *   that I may enter through them*
> *   and give thanks to the LORD.*

PSALM 119: *Marathon*

I run the way of your commandments,
for you enlarge my understanding.

This is the longest psalm of them all, 176 verses (the average psalm is ten or twenty), an almost vengeful length after the brief burst of Psalm 117. It feels like a test to get through it. It holds no great, unfolding dramatic story. Instead, it's a meditation on God's law, with emotional ups and downs about salvation and persecution and high-flying pledges from the psalmist that "I will keep your law continually, forever and ever."

The psalm urges the reader to walk with God, to find the way and stay the course on the journey. The very length of the psalm makes it a journey too, a challenge to stay on track without wandering. It's a marathon to read Psalm 119. There are literary reasons for its composition. It's an acrostic, using all the letters of the Hebrew alphabet—a mighty achievement, lost in English translation.

The resulting English contains beautiful passages, but the psalm threatens to bore. To declare something boring is the most damning denouncement you can make nowadays. A faith might be true, heaven and hell might be real; but if the package is a yawner, the audience will walk. The TV camera's pitiless demand, "Thou shalt not bore," is now the expectation for every public institution in politics, education, or worship. If the opposite of tedium is entertainment, then religion flirts with becoming Milli Vanilli, exciting today, a hapless, discredited relic tomorrow.

Reading Psalm 119 requires traits of the religious life itself—discipline, commitment, alertness to the big themes. Reading Psalm 119 will test muscles and build stamina, qualities that come in handy during the boring stretches, whether of worship or life.

I rise before dawn and cry for help;
I put my hope in your words.
My eyes are awake before each watch of the night,
that I may meditate on your promise.

Psalm 120: *Peacenik*

Too long have I had my dwelling
among those who hate peace.

S uddenly we're in a far-flung place, with a psalm writer longing for his
spiritual home, Jerusalem. He's far from native ground, far from peace
of mind. As far away as Meshech near the Black Sea or Kedar in southern
Arabia. He seems surrounded by warmongers: "I am for peace: but when I
speak, they are for war."

I attended a local peace vigil held for the plight of Tibet. People lit a
thousand candles to the cause of Tibetan Buddhism and the country's
political ordeal since 1950, when China invaded. The serene and smiling
Dalai Lama is the living symbol of Tibet's spiritual vibe and political cause.
Americans who knew little about Tibet went silently forward in a local
church to light a votive for world peace and diplomatic breakthroughs.

The campaign for Tibet is a phenomenon in this country. The themes of
Buddhist nonviolence and underdog status resonate with those who care
more for global justice and enlightenment than defense spending and tax
cuts. They find in the Tibetan cause an instant politico-spiritual community
otherwise hard to muster.

Talking to participants at such events, a reporter has to dig beyond the
solemn sloganeering for world peace and find the personal emotion burning
beneath. Everybody's for world peace; no news there. Press a person further
and you often discover that the Tibetan campaign, like any peace movement,
is not only a noble international cause but a way to articulate deeper yearnings for wholeness, healing, and the end to conflict in one's own life. The
moral issues at stake somehow speak to a specific condition or crisis in private life. The global and the personal meet.

The writer of Psalm 120, filled with the distress of exile, confidently
believes that God will hear his cry. A candle for a distant persecuted nation
is sometimes a candle for one's own inner exile in a society more at home
with aggression than with songs to peace.

Deliver me, O LORD,
from lying lips,
from a deceitful tongue.

PSALM 121: *Golden Slumbers*

He who keeps you will not slumber.

God is the God who never sleeps. God monitors every mood of life and nature, the daily flight of moon and stars, says Psalm 121: "The LORD is your keeper; the LORD is your shade at your right hand. The sun shall not strike you by day, nor the moon by night." God watches even as earth nightly takes a rest, when human life is most vulnerable, asleep. God beholds the settled-down scene, indeed holds it up. God is its keeper.

Years ago a theological movement got a lot of press and still smacks of titillation—the "death of God" movement. Taken literally it never made much sense. If God can die, then surely God never was God in the first place. And if God did die, surely the belief of millions—the poetry and the heat of their faith—would die too. It never has. The "death of God" crowd, a group of feisty theologians, had hoped to rattle the cage of establishment thinking. They wanted to throw out the traditional imagery of a remote transcendent God and find a better, more exciting way of talking about the presence of the divine in secular life. The movement was an affair of the city, dazzled by the all-night streetlights and choices of the modern urban scene where artificial distractions overwhelm the rhythms of human slumber and prayers. The city never sleeps, a spiritual condition far from the biblical world of shepherds and desert prophets.

The death of God movement never bothered to get out of town and climb a hill and lift its eyes upon those hills to search for answers that might be written in the star-heavy sky about the real life of God.

> *I lift up my eyes to the hills—*
>   *from where will my help come?*
> *My help comes from the LORD,*
>   *who made heaven and earth.*

PSALM 122: *Jerusalem Syndrome*

Pray for the peace of Jerusalem:
"May they prosper who love you."

We Nashvillians live in a religious town, the ornate buckle on the Bible belt, a busy major hub for American religion too. Located here are national religious publishing houses, theological schools, church agencies, contemporary Christian music makers, steeples everywhere.

The Protestant literature produced here sets the agenda for Sunday school discussions and sermons every week across the nation. The city's country music studios and bluegrass musicians keep a connection to memories of churchgoing, Bible-reading, sin, and redemption. And people come here to seek their music fortunes, feeling the guidance of the Lord. In such a city of dreams, ears stay cocked to every possibility of the voice of God.

So far, though, there's no mental condition officially known as "Nashville Syndrome." That phenomenon belongs only to one city in the world and always will: The Jerusalem Syndrome is a psychological state, much written about, that occasionally affects visitors or pilgrims to the holy city. These otherwise normal individuals wake up thinking they're a prophet or Jesus or some new messiah. They strip their clothes and wrap themselves in hotel bedsheets, if that, and shout suddenly urgent messages from the narrow streets. Once they leave Israel they're usually back to normal after a little therapy.

There is something disorienting and intoxicating about Jerusalem—the pink tones of the ancient stones at sunset, every little alleyway haunted by biblical history and all-too-real political agonies, the crossroad of three world religions. Psalm 122, a pilgrim song, celebrates the absolute sanctity of the place, which was overpowering even five hundred years before Christ. It has seen unspeakable wonders and horrors before and since then—accumulations of holiness that move pilgrims to helpless tears and prayers as recorded in Psalm 122.

I was glad when they said to me,
"Let us go to the house of the LORD!"
Our feet are standing within your gates, O Jerusalem.

PSALM 123: *Class*

Our soul has had more than its fill
of the scorn of those who are at ease,
of the contempt of the proud.

In Psalm 123 the writer lifts up his eyes in search of relief—relief from degradation, the contempt of the proud and haughty: "So our eyes look to the Lord our God, until he has mercy upon us."

This is the everyday experience of the have-nots encountering the haves. They're shut out, silenced, ignored. That's one way the haves feel good about themselves, by putting down the lowly, putting down the already put-down.

Often it's a class thing. In America no one comfortably talks about it. Differences of background, education, money, and opportunity drive painful wedges between people. It's a taboo subject, contradicting the very principle of our country's foundations: All are created equal. So people pretend the principle is in force: "Elitist" is about the worst thing you can call an American.

But class is real in society and in religion. The much-lamented divisions in religion usually relate to differences in neighborhood demographics. Theologies evolve to accommodate class instincts and distinctions—differences in worship aesthetics, social anxieties, pulpit humor.

Such differences are inevitable. But denying their existence does not make the quest for religious unity any easier. Denial makes it hard to hear news from those who feel hurt, who feel the contempt of privilege. In a biblical religion that proclaims every individual to be of sacred worth, the goal for all is to lift up their eyes, in unison—not with some looking down on others.

Have mercy upon us, O LORD, have mercy upon us,
for we have had more than enough of contempt.

PSALM 124: *Proof*

If it had not been the LORD who was on our side,
  when our enemies attacked us,
then they would have swallowed us up alive.

"Why is there something instead of nothing?" is a perennial question in books of philosophy. It leads to a classic answer, a logical proof for God's existence: that is, the creation of existence, so unnecessary, must have been the act of a willful Creator. (Who created the Creator? The questions are endless here on earth.)

Philosophical argument is noble and heroic, yet a bit comical too, as if proving God's existence rationally in any way changes the facts of daily life. We still have to get up in the morning and make a thousand judgment calls a day. The pristine arguments in the textbook are met with the epic silences of earth and sky. Anxious prayers continue whether we know Anselm's ontological proof or not. Rational proofs have little to do with the needs of the heart.

Writer Aldous Huxley supplied another sort of proof when he argued in his novel *Point Counterpoint* that a late Beethoven quartet, Opus 132, is so beautiful that it constitutes proof of God's reality. Author Walker Percy, a Catholic, set his proof for the existence of God not in philosophy or chamber music but in a people, the Jews. He said the survival of the Jews miraculously proves God's providential and mysterious guidance in the world. Somehow an obscure band of ancient Hebrews survived, claiming a covenant with the God of the universe, giving the world ethical principles and concepts of individual dignity and a sabbath day of rest. Meanwhile, all the mighty kingdoms of the ancient world turned to dust. "Where are the Hittites?" Percy asked. "Show me one Hittite living in New York City."

Psalm 124 is a homage of thanksgiving, a pause of gratitude for the survival of God's chosen people: "Our help is in the name of the LORD, who made heaven and earth." It's all the proof they needed.

Blessed be the LORD,
  who has not given us
  as prey to their teeth.

PSALM 125: *Fickle*

As the mountains surround Jerusalem,
so the LORD surrounds his people,
from this time on and forevermore.

G od remains as sturdy as the hills surrounding Jerusalem, Psalm 125 confides. Human life is just the opposite—fickle, impatient, bloodthirsty. Jerusalem has been a world stage of human hope and torment for millennia; the weary victim of siege, revolution, triumph, and defeat century after century; occupied by Assyrians, Babylonians, Greeks, Romans, Turks, British, Arabs, Zionists.

From time to time, psalmists complain of God's unpredictable comings and goings. Other times the Bible severely suggests otherwise: God is constant; humanity stumbles. Our homemade theologies come and go in embarrassing succession. God as stern judge or patient friend, God as holy wind or inner light, God as distant clock maker or evolving spirit—all these make up a history of fitful human attempts to say something fleeting about God with words blindly slanted by intellectual fashions and prejudices.

All the while the holy hills around Jerusalem continue their watch, unmoved by human theories, enthusiasms, and murderous instabilities. In the end religion comes down not to the latest theory of God but the ethics of behavior done in God's name. Psalm 125 states: "Do good, O LORD, to those who are good, and to those who are upright in their hearts."

Nothing fancy about that. Nothing fancy either about God's constancy, a notion and a hope as timeless as the hills.

Those who trust in the LORD are like Mount Zion,
which cannot be moved, but abides forever.

Psalm 126: *Sheaves*

Those who go out weeping,
bearing the seed for sowing,
shall come home with shouts of joy,
carrying their sheaves.

Bringing in the Sheaves" is one of those old-time hymns, nostalgic as an Andy Griffith rerun. The hymn symbolizes all that is remote about old-time religion. Its vocabulary (what are sheaves?) harkens back to farm-work and harvest gratitudes that few people grasp anymore. (A sheaf is a bundle of stalks or other crop material gathered at harvest time.)

In a culture no longer intimate with life on the farm and the rhythms and hazards of the growing season, prayers that ask for God's blessings over the land are an abstract exercise. In the city and its sprawling suburbs, prayer circles focus on matters closer to home—schoolyard safety, for instance, or the salvation of Hollywood.

A few years ago forty thousand people showed up for a local, downtown March for Jesus. They prayed for everything from the evils of pornography and racism to the hypocrisies of the country music business. No mention of bringing in the sheaves or rejoicing thereof.

The Bible, full of agricultural reference, situates its people firmly in a farming world. Contemporary society congratulates itself on being far beyond all that: a global economy too fast and furious for biblical nostalgia. But what if the Bible's agricultural wisdom—the sense of human dependence on God's blessing, a slowed-down savoring of the pleasures of soil and sun—is the intended moral yardstick for human life?

The question isn't welcome. Some churches now look like malls. Ample parking (asphalt where farmland used to be) is a big draw. But as long as there's an outdoors and an earth beneath the feet, someone will be bringing in the sheaves from somewhere, whether people think it's cool or not, so the world can eat.

Then our mouth was filled with laughter,
and our tongue with shouts of joy. . . .
The LORD has done great things for us,
and we rejoiced.

PSALM 127: *Children*

Lo, children are a heritage of the LORD (KJV).

In fewer than twenty lines Psalm 127 touches on three of life's consuming activities—making a home, raising children, getting sleep. There's a connection among them all.

Sleeplessness we associate both with raising kids and with trying to meet the mortgage payment. But this psalm says don't worry so much: "It is in vain that you rise up early and go late to rest, eating the bread of anxious toil."

Social commentators have wryly remarked about the pitiless arithmetic of three large modern pursuits—spending time, spending money, and owning a house. That is, it's hard to have all three at once. If you have money and a house, you never have time. If you have time and the house, you probably don't have much money.

Throw in the children and the math changes again—a further subtraction of time and money, an addition of new capacities for love and home-making. Parents know the joy of sitting in the house late at night, when the place is tranquil with the sound of their safe, sleeping children.

Lest couples without children think this short psalm has nothing for them, verse 1 boldly declares: "Unless the LORD builds the house, those who build it labor in vain. Unless the LORD guards the city, the guard keeps watch in vain."

Making a home filled with decency and a city with justice, a life free of anxiety, is the business of the (well-rested) human family.

For he gives sleep to his beloved.

PSALM 128: *Simplify*

Happy is everyone who fears the LORD,
*   who walks in his ways.*

F ear God and be blessed, Psalm 128 urges. We don't need an expert to
    grasp this simple wisdom. It's a rebuke to a thousand complicated ser-
mons. Fear God and be blessed. Find a companionable spouse, the psalm
encourages; raise children rightly; keep work simple and honest so you can
eat from the labor of your hands: "Happy shalt thou be, and it shall be well
with thee" (KJV).

Keep it simple. Follow the commandments. Avoid the snares and cruelties of power, wealth, fame. Stay out of debt. Avoid complicated schemes. Be
able to look people in the eye and tell the truth. Telling the truth is simpler
than lying. Lying requires that you remember all the previous lies you've told,
and to whom, in order to keep the lines of deceit humming and working.
Lying requires too much prodigious memory.

Fear of God means avoiding ambitions that compromise the Ten Commandments and endlessly complicate life. It means resisting choices that cor-
rupt, that promote lying, stealing, lusting. The simple life acknowledges a simple truth—serenity springs directly from a person's choices. So does misery.
This short, uncomplicated psalm carries no anguished complaint. Its tone is
serene. Some commentators believe it was sung by pilgrims going to Jerusalem at festival time.

The spiritual search today claims interest in simplicity, in unified theories
of living. Simplicity carries a certain humility with it. But it's hard to market
humility. Economic success depends on gregarious contacts and hustle and
promotional skills to sell the latest gadget, the latest formula of redemption.

Many a weekend seminar and Web site are devoted to finding the secret
of simplicity. It can get expensive. It might be simpler all around to discover
the secret in Psalm 128.

You shall eat the fruit of the labor of your hands;
*   you shall be happy,*
and it shall go well with you.

PSALM 129: *Peace Be with You*

The blessing of the LORD be upon you!

Years ago the worshipers at my church started "exchanging the peace," a tradition where people greet one another in the name of the Lord halfway through the service. "Peace be with you," we were asked to say. It was awkward at first. Some refused completely, staring straight ahead, arms folded in that cold, uncomfortable-in-church way. The idea of turning around to shake hands with a stranger and say priestly sounding words—wasn't that the minister's job? Who were we to enact such a blessing?

Others really got in to it, wandering away from their pew to bear hug friends and strangers alike. It's sound theology and good faith to acknowledge the people around you during worship. Otherwise it's possible to sit for an hour and a half singing hymns and saying creeds together but never looking at the person beside or behind you—for the next forty years.

Psalm 129 is early evidence of such a worship-assembly greeting. The peace-blessing comes at the end of a short bitter recollection of the history of the sufferings of Israel: "The plowers plowed on my back; they made their furrows long."

At church, the words of blessing carry a certain heft and power. It's a physical way of claiming a sliver of the wind and movement of God and showing a little transcendent courtesy on a sabbath morn.

More and more congregations are adding this blessing, this practice, regularly to their worship settings. They all go through the initial shyness. Soon enough the words take root. They become a fondly awaited part of the service, turning bitter psalms of experience into a common ground of faith among strangers.

> *"The blessing of the LORD be upon you!*
> *We bless you in the name of the LORD!"*

PSALM 130: *Come Morning*

I wait for the LORD, my soul waits,
and in his word I hope.

I n the religious life, people live by paradox. We say God is with us, yet in a
deeper sense we wait for God.

God is with us in the Communion bread and wine or in the reading of
Torah or in the thrilled calling down of the Holy Spirit. But these experiences usually end at the close of worship or when the Good Book is shut.

Then the waiting commences again—the waiting for wisdom, consola-
tion, and an ultimate visitation that will transform earth and soul for good
and forever. Psalm 130 comes at us not with conventional cheer but in turmoil: "Out of the depths I cry to you, O LORD."

Waiting is no easy sell. In the competition among faiths, bonus points go
to pragmatic sermons and uplift, not prolonged waiting. The Quakers are a
notable exception for the way they enshrine and ennoble waiting, giving
over whole services to sitting in silence, waiting. No one speaks unless the
spirit moves a person to words.

The writer of Psalm 130 waits passionately. It's not embarrassed or
defeated waiting, but it is waiting nevertheless. It takes courage. Waiting suggests you don't have all the answers. The psalm writer says his hope resides in
God's word during the wait. The word is the covered shelter in the rain, the
book to open while waiting for the rainbow at the end of the storm.

My soul waits for the Lord
more than those who watch for the morning,
more than those who watch for the morning.

PSALM 131: *Bone Weary*

O LORD, my heart is not lifted up,
  my eyes are not raised too high.

Some psalms are full of extravagant praise of the Almighty and certainty of being on God's side. Psalm 131 sets those emotions aside, exhausted. The mood has drastically shifted. The writer, emptied of grand and lofty ambitions, seems disillusioned. Perhaps he has experienced a terrible setback or is just plain bone-tired.

Whatever the reason, the psalmist is humble, quiet, a person of few words. Psalm 131 is but a dozen lines or so offered in a minor key. The psalmist isn't up for lots of theology or long banquet prayers. He's content to acknowledge his spiritual limits: "I do not occupy myself with things too great and too marvelous for me."

The psalm writer says memorably, "But I have calmed and quieted my soul, like a weaned child with its mother; my soul is like the weaned child that is with me." His soul is weaned away from what? Possibly he has had his fill of battle or politics or sanctified struggle. He's burned out, trying to take new breath without the hot air of overblown sentences that wrap a person in haughtiness or boundless boasts of divine insight.

For some reason the psalmist feels cut down to size, human size. He doesn't resist. He keeps the psalm short. He exits the scene with his human voice intact and his eyes on something larger than himself.

O Israel, hope in the LORD
  from this time on and forevermore.

Psalm 132: *Ark*

Rise up, O LORD, and go to your resting place,
you and the ark of your might.

On the religion beat you soon run into people in search of the Lost Ark—a whole subculture of adventurers, usually Americans, who read their Bible and have a taste for mountainous Mideast terrain. They're determined to find the ark—Noah's ark, that is, or the ark of the covenant or both.

Mainstream scholarship long ago concluded that both arks are lost to history, impossible to recover. Ark searchers, eager to prove the Bible true, scoff at such pessimism. They use sonar and satellite photos to legitimize the science of their search. In the end they never quite come up with evidence that keeps the world's attention for long.

One amateur I met boasted that he had found not just one ark but both of them, the archaeological jackpot of the millennium. He was waiting for the right moment to reveal them to the world. His secrets died with him a few years ago.

It's an American style of Bible reading: A person reads a verse and thinks the clues are right before her eyes, freeze-dried or freshly minted and waiting just for her despite four millennia of dusty history, countless digs, and many generations of careful scholarship.

Psalm 132 is the only psalm that mentions the ark of the covenant. The ark, a wooden chest of holy contents enshrined with utmost reverence, contained the stone tablets of Moses, Aaron's rod, and pieces of manna from the days of the Israelites' early wanderings. The Hebrews carried it into the Promised Land with them, and it rested in a gilded place in Solomon's temple.

By the sixth century B.C.E, the ark of the covenant had vanished. The sacking of Jerusalem by Israel's enemies might explain its disappearance, but the Bible is vague on the subject. It's as if the Bible is saying: Give it up. Treasure hunts won't prove anything. Faith is not something you find with a pickax and hold in your hand and use as a ticket to fame.

Let your priests be clothed with righteousness,
and let your faithful shout for joy.

PSALM 133: *Oily*

How very good and pleasant it is
*   when kindred live together in unity!*
It is like the precious oil on the head,
*   running down upon the beard.*

P recious oils running down the length of the body, dripping from head and beard, trickling to the skirts of garments—such sensuality is rare enough in life or religion. Yet it dominates Psalm 133. Images of dew and oil all celebrate the theme of unity, togetherness. It seems a surprising way to hail such an unglamorous religious virtue—unity—that otherwise never gets much credit.

The twentieth century, reportedly the era of religious unity, enjoyed ecumenical successes for a while. Official dialogues between denominations were begun. Some religious bodies merged, having outlived or forgotten why they split in the first place.

Other denominations declined to join the excitement. They preferred to carry on alone. They invested their integrity and identity in a highly cultivated separateness. Nationally more than forty-five hundred separate religious bodies all thrive by carving up the world and claiming their own slice. They have their own constituencies. They were doing niche marketing before the secular world ever dreamed of it.

Some commentators say the unity noted in Psalm 133 revolves around a specific property issue in ancient Israel, a plea to keep families together so the inherited ancestral land is not split up and threatened. In a modern worship setting far from debates about inheritance laws in ancient Israel, we use Psalm 133 to declare the virtue of communal unity and common-ground values of the Golden Rule, the love of God, and scripture.

But until we view unity as fun-filled and as holy as pouring a bottle of anointed oil on your head, no one's going to get terribly excited.

It is like the dew of Hermon,
*   which falls on the mountains of Zion.*
For there the LORD ordained his blessing,
*   life forevermore.*

PSALM 134: *Liftoff*

Lift up your hands to the holy place, and bless the LORD.

A big church split took place in town because some people raised their hands during worship. They didn't steal money or molest anybody. They raised their hands as an expression of joy or piety, which had never been done before. People could legitimately use their hands for prayer or for hugs, handshakes, and pulpit gestures but not for raising during worship from the pews. To the outsider, raised hands look innocuous, a bizarre reason for a cataclysmic split in a century-old congregation. Outsiders always underestimate the megaton power of religious tradition.

Inside the church, the non-hand raisers considered hand raising to be a sign of emotional excess, a Pentecostal flourish and a suspect faith. It's guilt by association. Those who raise their hands were seen as insurrectionists from the other team, sowers of discord.

For two hundred years people didn't raise their hands in "respectable" worship. But today public life is convulsing with change. Emotion, confession, and grief go public now. At worship a decline in formality and decorum is explained by the influence of pop music and consumerism—or the unstoppable spirit of God. Some hand raisers are indeed new Pentecostalists hoping to incite change in a staid congregation. Others simply find permission in this psalm to raise their hands as an apt expression of the moment.

In a politicized climate no innocent gestures remain. A hug can be misinterpreted in the gender wars. A raised hand can bring up sudden questions of theology and allegiance.

Naming enemies, choosing sides, and demanding loyalty to old ways or new gets people's juices flowing. Personally, though, the older I get, the less use I have for these overheated conflicts. Divisions, polemics, and culture wars are an industry, an addiction, a lucrative and self-serving patter in an era of incessant news updates. I'd rather "stand by night," as this short psalm proposes, "in the house of the LORD."

Come, bless the LORD, all you servants of the LORD,
who stand by night in the house of the LORD!

PSALM 135: *Breathless*

The idols of the nations are silver and gold,
*   the work of human hands.*
They have mouths, but they do not speak;
*   they have eyes, but they do not see; . . .*
and there is no breath in their mouths.

Psalm 135 resembles a lecture that reviews material before the big test. We've heard these themes before. God the all-powerful, the psalm writer reminds, is not an idol. God is not a stone object to be worshiped, not a lifeless figurine finite and corruptible. Idols are destined to crack, disappoint, and return to dust, rather like people.

No, this God is not to be confused with any elements of finite earth. This God is infinite. God made the wind, but we can't see God's breath, for breath is a sign of mortal life. The stirrings of breath will one day cease. Breath doesn't last. This God does: "For I know that the LORD is great; our Lord is above all gods."

The carriers of this faith, mere mortals, have this privilege and responsibility: Use words and music to remember God's name, God's code of ethics, and the stories of divine dealings with people.

Over and over, Psalm 135 urges us to bless the Lord and remember the Lord's name. Feel the wind, this psalm lecturer instructs. Think of the great adventure of creation and its Maker. But be not dazzled by silver, gold, and other counterfeit enticements.

Class dismissed.

Your name, O Lord, endures forever,
*   your renown, O Lord, throughout all ages.*
For the Lord will vindicate his people,
*   and have compassion on his servants.*

PSALM 136: 24/7

For his steadfast love endures forever.

Perplexities await the world every morning. High on the list is the question of God's actual presence in our personal lives and the earth itself. What is it and where?

Psalm 136 recites a litany of God's mighty acts on behalf of ancient Israel. Whether creating the world itself or destroying Israel's enemies, God intervenes with ease across nature and history in the eyes of faith.

But these events are set in the remote past. What about today? Believers work out their own understanding God's action. Three basic attitudes toward God's acts prevail:

- God acted mightily in past history. God doesn't act in those distinct ways anymore for God's own reasons. Some Christians say God's abiding stage of action today is the church; that's where God acts. Some Jews seek God's power and presence in the words and sinews of the holy scrolls of Torah, the Law.
- God's actions take place in the here and now—in the private lives of believers who experience miracles, divine coincidences, and moments of grace.
- God's action is embodied in one basic observation every day—the existence of the world. God created the world and sustains it. *Sustain* is a verb that barely conveys the unbelievable act of upholding all life in the universe and the cosmos itself, twenty-four hours a day, the guts and structures of time too. The most striking part of Psalm 136 is the refrain, repeated twenty-six times. It serves as a testimony to this continuous miracle: "For his steadfast love endures forever."

Compared to that sustenance, any specific miraculous intervention of God seems like icing on the cake.

It is he who remembered us in our low estate,
for his steadfast love endures forever.

PSALM 137: *Notorious*

Happy shall they be who take your little ones
and dash them against the rock!

At last we come to the most notorious passage in the book of Psalms, the savage, nauseating reference to the brutal killing of little children. Skeptics quote it to challenge the Bible's suitability as an ethical guide. I dreaded getting to Psalm 137. Reading it now, my emotions are more complicated than simple dread.

Psalm 137 reads like an eyewitness account to a national catastrophe, the fall of Jerusalem to the Babylonians. The "fall of Jerusalem" is a bland, shorthand phrase that hardly touches on the blood and screaming terror of the event—hostile soldiers laying siege to the city, attacking the walls, killing leaders, starving the inhabitants, dragging thousands of people away in captivity, and burning the place to the ground.

Now imprisoned far east of his homeland by mocking oppressors, the psalm writer moans, "For there our captors asked us for songs, and our tormentors asked for mirth, saying, 'Sing us one of the songs of Zion!'"

The rest of the psalm is a procession of regret and sorrow, then a pledge to remember Jerusalem and return once more. It pours contempt on the people who caused Jerusalem such suffering. Human emotion seethes: "Happy shall they be who pay you back what you have done to us! Happy shall they be who take your little ones and dash them against the rock!"

It's a cry of deepest frustration and agony. We cannot prettify or spiritualize it. The verse is disgusting. The verse is a litmus test in the battle over the Bible. Conservative readers say the Bible is true in its entirety. Skeptics ridicule that attitude by pointing to the immorality of this passage. But what does the passage mean? The verse arrives as an angry outburst, not a murderous official executive order to be carried out. We don't know if it actually happened. We don't know if it's true. But it reads like an authentically human cry, uncensored, one more voice in the thickly textured biblical drama of God's dealings with impatient, murderous humanity.

By the rivers of Babylon—
there we sat down and there we wept
when we remembered Zion.

Psalm 138: *Fly*

For though the LORD is high, he regards the lowly;
but the haughty he perceives from far away.

From Sunday school on, we're told God loves us more than we can imagine or know, a perfect love because God knows us transcendently and loves us unconditionally. Then when God doesn't always come to the rescue, we're disappointed. Evil happens or stupid little things happen that God could have stopped, and we wonder whether God loves us at all. Some folks conclude, drastically, that God is out to get us and has renounced us as unworthy in some final, cosmic way.

Psalm 138 reveals no misgivings: "I give you thanks, O LORD, with my whole heart; before the gods I sing your praise." The reference to "gods" is another bit of the old polytheism that the Bible sometimes acknowledges. But another image prevails—praise rising above the tumble of daily life, past the slings and arrows, past the whims of other "gods" or forces that exert control over the earth (money, lobbyists, tornadoes, e-mail viruses, drought, mail-order catalogs).

Praising God revives the soul. That's the medicine prescribed in Psalm 138. That perfect love, which we've been hearing about since childhood, survives the assaults of life and death, that final card life plays on us.

Psalm 138 is a hymn of praise that flies upward, hoping to reach its destination, our destiny.

> *Though I walk in the midst of trouble,*
> *you preserve me against the wrath of my enemies;*
> *you stretch out your hand,*
> *and your right hand delivers me.*

PSALM 139: *Overpowering Idea*

> *If I ascend to heaven, you are there;*
> *if I make my bed in Sheol, you are there.*

In Psalm 139 we seem to witness a psalm writer thinking his way to a new position, a new clarity about God's power and all-knowingness: "If I take the wings of the morning and settle at the farthest limits of the sea, even there your hand shall lead me, and your right hand shall hold me fast." The psalm declares there's nothing you can hide from God, nowhere you can escape—not even in death.

Psalm 139 seems to conflict with Psalm 6:5, which says, "For in death there is no remembrance of you." By now the sheer logic of an overpowering idea, God's omnipotence, pushes the writer into new mental territory: Nothing is out of reach of this God, not even the shadowy afterworld, whether it's called Sheol or the pit of hell.

The notion that ideas evolve in scripture might sound questionable, uncomfortable. Evolving ideas suggest that earlier knowledge was faulty or correctable—or, to look at it another way, slowly revealed in God's good time.

Hell seems to be an unfolding concept in the Bible. Early on, the afterlife is a dim destination, Sheol, the place of both the righteous and unrighteous. By Jesus' time, hell represents an everlasting pit of torment for the wicked. Since then, theologians have argued it all over the map:

- Hell is agonized separation from God, in this life or the next.
- Hell is rented space: Perhaps people land there for a while, but eventually everyone ends up in heaven.
- Hell is a concept repulsive to a loving God. Hell may indeed exist, but it is empty.

The psalm writer feels passionately convicted that God embraces all knowledge and all whereabouts. The writer has little time for cautious theological hairsplitting as he squints mightily in the intense glow of omnipotence, which is more than anyone can fathom. Psalm 139 admits as much:

> *How weighty to me are your thoughts, O God!*
> . . . .
> *Such knowledge is too wonderful for me;*
> *it is so high that I cannot attain it.*

PSALM 140: *Deliver Me*

Guard me, O LORD, from the hands of the wicked;
*   protect me from the violent*
*   who have planned my downfall.*

Psalm 140 gives the floor to a wounded voice. The reader wants to turn away, but the voice isn't leaving. The psalm writer is in a complaining mood. Enemies abound. He fantasizes about their death and pleads to God to vindicate his vengeful desire.

The psalm is unapologetic, unseemly, self-involved. The writer wants God to blast his personal enemies immediately. He's too impatient to wait for justice in the afterlife. He wants satisfaction now. Soon he reveals a clue to his situation: He's an outcast, maybe part of a social underclass, struggling against scorn: "I know that the LORD maintains the cause of the needy, and executes justice for the poor."

Some readers will pass over this psalm and declare it inferior to many others because of its vindictiveness. Old Testament scholar Bernhard W. Anderson, in his book *Out of the Depths: The Psalms Speak for Us Today*, cautions against hasty negative judgments on such psalms. Marginalized people, mistreated by prejudice or institutional powers, can relate to psalms of complaint and give voice to them.

Everyone knows such marginal neighborhoods where sagging little churches can't pay the minister much, and the city can't find the money to beautify that part of town or to repave the road, and the nonprofit foundation has no grant for the kids' art projects, and tax-cut prosperity never finds its way to their address. Out of their mouths, Psalm 140's harsh plea carries unheard authority.

The arrogant have hidden a trap for me,
*   and with cords they have spread a net,*
*   along the road they have set snares for me.*

I say to the LORD, "You are my God;
*   give ear, O LORD, to the voice of my supplications."*

PSALM 141: *Incensed*

Let my prayer be counted as incense before you.

I ncense is a misunderstood detail of religion. Many believers are suspicious of incense. It reminds them of Halloween or head shops or pagan rites and priestly darkness and alien incantations, highbrow hoodoo.

The real worry might be that incense is sensual. It's physical and has a smell. It's earthy (which is not far from "worldly"), which can lead to stray thoughts, carnal thoughts. It strikes the pious as something akin to lighting up in the holy place—smoking of any kind shouldn't be allowed in God's house.

Long before Protestantism sprang up from Europe's religious malaise, incense was used with utmost sanctity as a sign of God's holiness, a symbol of the worshipers' prayers rising to heaven. The ancient Israelites used incense in Temple worship (perhaps to cover the stench of sacrificed animals.) Later, the Magi could think of no greater gift for a newborn savior than frankincense.

Other sensual, touchable details envelop Psalm 141: "Set a guard over my mouth, O LORD; keep watch over the door of my lips. Do not turn my heart to any evil, . . . do not let me eat of their delicacies." Other images abound: oils, stony places, scattered bones, lifted hands.

Incense at worship time isn't the main issue and never was. It symbolizes the psalmist's lavish request of God to keep him in righteousness and wisdom: "In you I seek refuge; do not leave me defenseless."

Incense also reminds me that faith is not simply an affair of the abstract mind. The smell of incense argues that religious practice does not ban the physical senses. The scent is a reminder of breath, the fact that people bring their breathing bodies with them to worship. The Bible declares that God is God of the living.

I call upon you, O LORD; come quickly to me;
give ear to my voice when I call to you.

PSALM 142: *Prison Term*

Look on my right side and see—
*   there is no one who takes notice of me;*
no refuge remains to me;
no one cares for me.

Psalm 142 delivers a heap of trouble. The odor of isolation is overpowering—a scenario of a person imprisoned, no friend left, no one to take notice, a human spirit fading and fainting.

For nearly three hundred years Western philosophy has concluded that we're all imprisoned in our own subjectivity, our own faulty cognitive filters on the world, which makes the discovery of objective truth impossible. Of course, the strange irony is that these dire conclusions are carefully written down and published in books: The entire assumption of the writing and production of books is that words can be communicated and shared with a world of readers. To write a book at all is to deny the smug dictum that no truth can be told or attempted.

For every pessimistic philosophical conclusion, there is a counterargument or counterintuition made by every human being on earth who has ever gotten up in the morning and attended to the thousand tasks that confront him or her as parent, spouse, breadwinner, homeowner, citizen, mentor, friend, or believer. The truth is, we live every day as if truth exists and can be grasped and communicated and acted on despite every self-delusion and boneheaded mistake.

The writer of Psalm 142, back against the wall, cries out to God, the last and best chance he has. Anyone who has despaired in the dark—hammered by isolation, imprisoned in shame or regret or hopelessness—has uttered that cry: "I cry to you, O LORD; I say, 'You are my refuge, my portion in the land of the living.'"

And when answers come, whether apprehended in the nick of time or the fullness of time, they scandalize philosophy, which will never admit to making sense of the psalmist's final words:

Bring me out of prison,
*   so that I may give thanks to your name.*
The righteous will surround me,
*   for you will deal bountifully with me.*

PSALM 143: *Muddle*

I remember the days of old,
I think about all your deeds,
I meditate on the works of your hands.
I stretch out my hands to you;
my soul thirsts for you like a parched land.

We might think of the Bible as the good ole days, when spiritual heroes walked the earth. Yet even the Bible, as reflected in Psalm 143, expresses nostalgia for way-back-when, when times were better, faith was stronger, God's presence was sure.

Here we are, rounding the backstretch to the monumental collection of Psalms, and still the voice cries out: "Answer me quickly, O LORD; my spirit fails. Do not hide your face from me."

The human condition limps on. Nothing has changed since the night this psalm was sung with hopes that the night would pass: "Let me hear of your steadfast love in the morning, for in you I put my trust." Morning light will give the psalmist his bearings again.

We never resolve this struggle between fear and faith. Some grow impatient with it, wearying of the struggle and tension. They want it over and done with. They want Armageddon. They want the Messiah to come within the hour, nirvana in the afternoon. They're on the verge of divinity and ready to burst. No one can live with that pressure for long. The human vessel isn't built to hold apocalypse now.

Occasionally there's a rapture scare in America: Believers work up unearthly hopes that Jesus will soon return; and they will vanish in thin air, swooped up in deathless transport to heaven. They quit their jobs and give away possessions to those who will be left behind.

Disappointment comes when the skies do not open, not yet. Truth has not yet been fulfilled. They'll have to wait, which means dealing with tomorrow and its unpredictable moods, the need for sleep and food, new pleasures and annoyances. The search for ultimate contentment isn't finished. It's future-oriented, future-tilted. Ultimate contentment arrives in a foreign country called the future.

Teach me to do your will,
for you are my God.

PSALM 144: *Music City*

I will sing a new song to you, O God;
upon a ten-stringed harp I will play to you.

Psalm 144 reached back to images of the music-making King David and forward even to the latter-day bluegrass festivals of the American South. It urgently commemorates two themes: the fragile brevity of life and praise of eternal God.

Here in Nashville, a capital of music and religion, both these insights converge. The bluegrass music around here catalogs the sorrows of this passing life, the vain flashy briefness of it all amid God's mysterious will. The music itself—voice, guitar, fiddle, banjo, mandolin, dobro—serves as a consoling choir for this condition of impermanence, a way to mark time and offer catharsis for nightmares and nameless longings.

The psalm writer knew the potency of music. King David famously picked up an instrument of ten strings and made sounds that would echo and vibrate into the indefinite future of faith. Listeners pick up some of the vibrations whenever the Stanley Brothers or Emmylou Harris sings a song about this mortal coil. Any bluegrass gathering on a Saturday night—in a barn outside of town or in a downtown honky-tonk—will make contact with that deep pool of sadness and praise.

At this moment, the NASA *Voyager* probe is angling into deep space, carrying a gold CD recording of the sounds of earthlings in case it encounters intelligent life with a good ear. The CD includes sounds of nature and a long list of snatches of music—Bach, Beethoven, a Navajo chant, "Johnny B. Goode"—but apparently no old mountain tunes or spirituals that testify in their special way to a certain gut-bucket, baseline human condition, the prison of mortality, a God to praise, a melody to convey the sweet sadness of it all.

It's been said that poetry attempts to say something permanent about impermanence. So does music, the sound track of life's long, strange journey.

Happy are the people to whom such blessings fall;
happy are the people whose God is the LORD.

PSALM 145: *Slammed*

Every day I will bless you,
and praise your name forever and ever.

People have time. We say we don't. But we do. We have time to do what we choose to do every day. We complain about the lack of time. Yet somehow we find time to endure every modern delay. People have time to sit in line at the car wash all morning. There's time to stare indefinitely at the computer screen while the files download ever so slowly. There's time for airline delays and for waiting an hour for a table at the Friday-night restaurant.

We stay busy, and we let others know it. That way we can feel important in the new economy. Slowing down is intolerable. The toilet is an intrusion. Death itself becomes the ultimate annoying interruption, the forced career move, the unscheduled cosmic impertinence.

The busy person who glances at Psalm 145 will get a good chuckle: "I will extol you, my God and King, and bless your name forever and ever," and "Every day I will bless you." Every day? Who's got the time? "On the glorious splendor of your majesty, and on your wondrous works, I will meditate." Can I reschedule? I am just so slammed right now.

The biggest urban legend going is to say there's no time. There's time. The day adds up to a hundred decisions, priorities, goals, choices. Every morning we rack them up and pick through them again.

Psalm 145 piles up the activity, lots of verbs, a full plate of praise to God— "One generation shall laud your works to another, and shall declare your mighty acts," and "They shall speak of the glory of your kingdom, and tell of your power. " And God communicates back—"You open your hand, satisfying the desire of every living thing."

Technology has allowed us to cram more and more into our heads and our lives. Outrageously, each day still contains just twenty-four hours. We can regard that as a limit that mocks us daily or an extraordinary gift to accept. People have time, time for praise—if it's important enough. People have time. It's all we have.

The LORD is near to all who call on him,
to all who call on him in truth.

PSALM 146: *Party of God*

Do not put your trust in princes,
in mortals, in whom there is no help.

Psalm 146 resides deep in the political world, always a dangerous place. It lists characteristics and actions that God values on earth: God stands for the oppressed, the hungry, the imprisoned. God preserves the strangers, relieves the fatherless and widows, loves the righteous, cuts off the wicked. It adds up to an unavoidable social agenda. It requires planning, stamina, implementation—all in the political realm—if it's going to be done.

Yet one message of this psalm is, Don't trust the political leaders; don't trust humanity. For generations, millions of Bible believers in America were political pessimists who stayed out of political frays as a matter of belief. Some refused to vote, choosing not to sully their faith with worldly machinations.

Some believers take the opposite extreme now, setting themselves up as the Party of God to implement God's will and purposes. They hang out only with people like themselves, rejecting larger coalitions and viewpoints. The world is blistering with Party of God operatives now.

Psalm 146 poses a quandary. It suggests God's agenda for human life is ambitious and absolute. There's much work to be humanly done on earth. Yet the psalm says humans are not trustworthy in any ultimate way. What's the way out of the quandary? Check another psalm or two for advice. Psalm 103 sings of the importance of covenant. Covenant, as introduced in the Bible, is the link between heaven and earth. Covenant with God demands that people work for righteousness. In return, God is faithful to them.

Those who shun political solutions that help the hungry, the imprisoned, and the fatherless might recall that the marching orders come not from some party boss or newspaper editorial but from Yahweh, the Almighty.

The LORD sets the prisoners free;
the LORD opens the eyes of the blind.
The LORD lifts up those who are bowed down;
the LORD loves the righteous.

PSALM 147: *Remember*

He sends out his command to the earth;
his word runs swiftly.

We're wrapping things up. The end of the book of Psalms is near. Psalm 147 runs at a faster clip, as if to cram into place one last summary of God's attributes and powers. For nearly 150 psalms, the psalms have extolled God's miraculous deeds and declared God's tenderness. Psalm 147 recaps it all, a convenient patchwork of the acts of God, as if to say: Here are the themes of these psalms; you've heard them in voices of joy, agony, poetry; here they are once more. Remember them:

- Remember that God "determines the number of the stars; he gives to all of them their names."
- Remember that God "covers the heavens with clouds, prepares rain for the earth, makes grass grow on the hills."
- Remember that God "gives to the animals their food, and to the young ravens when they cry."
- Remember that God "grants peace within your borders; he fills you with the finest of wheat."
- Remember that God "lifts up the downtrodden; he casts the wicked to the ground."
- Remember that God "takes pleasure in those who fear him, in those who hope in his steadfast love."
- And remember to "make melody to our God on the lyre."

Remember these themes, the psalm urges. Behold how thorough is God's interest in the world. God reaches into intimate interiors, infinite exteriors. God's word "runs swiftly." The reading of God's word circles the globe, plants secret seeds.

Connect the dots. Consult the manual. This is God's world.

Great is our Lord, and abundant in power;
his understanding is beyond measure.

PSALM 148: *Dragons*

Praise the LORD from the earth,
*   you sea monsters and all deeps.*

There's no holding back now. All creation is there to sing divine praises. Everything has the capacity in its own strange or secret way. Everything gives off its own spiritual heat and luminosity to acknowledge God. Psalm 148 catalogs the entities of the universe, from top to bottom, the huge and the lowly, all enlisted in the praise of their Creator.

The list includes angels, sun, moon, shining stars, "waters above the heavens," fire, hail, snow, frost, stormy wind, mountains, hills, fruit trees, cedars, wild animals, cattle, creeping things, flying birds, kings of the earth, all peoples, princes, young and old, men, women, children—all a democracy of the spirit. Sea monsters too. The King James Version calls them *dragons*, a word that stirs mythical memories and childhood images ("Puff the Magic Dragon"). And a slight revulsion: It's hard to imagine deep-sea monsters giving praise to the biblical God. Aren't dragons supposed to be mean, sour, fire-breathing? Yet here they have their place.

The monsters have symbolic power. They represent darknesses lurking beneath human consciousness; the murky reptilian depths too scary to confront, where personal wounds and enlightenment are imprisoned. Arguably Psalm 148 admits their existence, vindicates their value as scaly bearers of wisdom. The poet Robert Bly describes this "shadow" material as the dark side—not evil but a side of human life that people prefer to postpone or ignore. Skip over it, says Bly, and it can destroy you. Ignore its existence—the passions you pack away there, the hurt memories, the guilt feelings, the creativity—and it doesn't go away. It erupts in distorted vindictive ways elsewhere in the personality.

So Psalm 148 puts monsters of the deep on the list, whatever they might be in this world. Praise of God isn't complete until they join the chorus.

Let them praise the name of the LORD,
*   for he commanded and they were created.*
He established them forever and ever;
*   he fixed their bounds, which cannot be passed.*

PSALM 149: *Double-Edged*

For the LORD takes pleasure in his people;
he adorns the humble with victory.

A party is going on in Psalm 149, a rising penultimate free-for-all of religious celebration. There's dancing and music-making, joined by the saints of glory and all Israel: "Let them sing for joy on their couches."

And yet even upon this remarkably festive, noisy scene of scripture, a sprig of bitter herb is added, the reminder that all is never festivity only: Belief in God also inspires opposition, disorder, resistance. Verses 6 and 7 are there to sober everybody up: "Let the high praises of God be in their throats and two-edged swords in their hands, to execute vengeance on the nations and punishment on the people."

Punishment for the scoffers of God is never far from the psychology of the Psalms. Revelers would rather not think about it. The momentum of exuberance tends to smooth things over, minimize the negative.

Psalm 149 arrives to say: Keep both eyes open; be wary of untruth. Full-throated praise is the main thing but don't go soft. There is always thinking to do, analysis, adult seriousness. The political world will raise up opposition. Be tough-minded. Acknowledge the hard realities. Don't sentimentalize or harmonize opposites too hastily.

This comes as difficult advice. People of faith are taught to be peace-makers, reconcilers. The world's story is full of paradox: It's God's world, the Psalms tell us; it's also a hazardous place. It's a world wired for the praise of God, operated by human beings gifted with choice. We can choose either to voice that praise or plot dramatic but futile resistance.

Sing to the LORD a new song,
his praise in the assembly of the faithful.

. . . .

This is glory for the faithful ones.

PSALM 150: *Cymbalism*

Let everything that breathes praise the LORD!

In the end, there is music, the music of praise. People congregate inside or swarm outside to stand beneath the firmament. No matter where they turn, they hear praise of God. Sounds of trumpet, pipe, and harp flood the air. Music blankets the hills, plains, and all breathing creatures, making every molecule hum. Music can accomplish what prayers and thoughts cannot quite do—flesh out the air with sonic colors, adding an extra language for answering the Creator, touching the creation with sound.

There's dance. Dance gives a person a dimension of expression beyond thoughts and words. Dance brings the body up to speed, involving it in a theology of the moment, enlisting it as an equal partner with the heart and the mind, those miraculous entities carried by the body. Dance allows body its moment in the sun despite an ancient reluctance of heart and mind to yield way to it.

And there are loud cymbals—nerve-wracking, magnificent, inevitable—like the word of God itself, bearing news of God's omnipotence and arrival. This is news unheard and unthought until unleashed through the reading of scripture, coming like the crashing cymbal of Psalm 150. That high-sounding cymbal sets the tone for the human parade of high-steppers and strugglers, all within earshot of the secret thunder and divine music arriving from the center of the Bible, the living sound of the book of Psalms.

Let everything that breathes praise the LORD!

AFTERWORD
The Never-Ending Story

To attend a spiritual retreat is to find a temporary antidote for a frantic world of long commutes, tiny work cubicles, and endless media jabber. Retreats offer a day's focus on nature poetry, journaling, meditation, or other strategies for weeding and watering the garden of the inner life. I've led a few local ones myself. No matter what the subject, a spiritual retreat follows a certain emotional pattern through the day. It has its own life cycle, its own DNA.

A retreat begins with preconceptions, eager expectations, a little apprehension or nervousness. By late morning, if the thing is going well, the itinerary reveals surprise, fascination, a new sense of community. After lunch, the rhythms shift again—now to a feeling of being midway on a long journey, terrain unknown. Fatigue and alertness battle for the upper hand.

By midafternoon, there's a turning. You're going home soon; you've covered more ground than you realized, with sheer personal stamina you didn't know you had. You've left behind some old assumptions or secondhand opinions. The texture of the world is a little richer for the twists and turns of this unusual day.

That's how it feels to work steadily through the 150 Psalms, like a retreat from business as usual, a distance measured not in miles and hours but in chapters and verses. It starts quietly at Psalm 1 near a tree by a stream, an outdoor metaphor for the word of God. It ends with music soaring to the praise of the Lord. At every turn, momentous emotions and images flood the horizon—thunderclaps, vistas of beauty, spells of drought, valleys, darkness, breakthrough, deliverance.

The Psalms beckon reader and writer to confront the words cold and discover what happens next—trace how the spirit of each psalm connects with this moment, then see what stirs and follow where it goes. The more I wrote, the bigger and closer the Bible got. At the same time, the many aggressive theories about biblical authority, liberal or conservative, became less and less relevant. Scripture's authority, its antiquity, its power to inhabit a reader today, elude explanation or reduction. The clamorous debates about the Bible fall into the deep background as you camp in the shadows of the

Psalms themselves. What matters more is the momentum, the adventure of reading and writing and the wonder or resolve that follows.

Sit down to write, and you tap into an internal dialogue, overhearing things about yourself or the world or faith that might never have surfaced otherwise. The Psalms provoke that interior drama. I started this project with a thousand questions about God. Over time, questions retreated as the divine mystery drew closer, like a vast ship in the dark. I can feel the wake of its movement, an undertow. The Psalms bring news of the life of God: Our very existence points to a Creator who remains constant, who watches, who overwhelms, who outwaits our own self-defeating moods and manias.

It's anyone's right and privilege to try this sequence of reading and writing and to assemble a personal memoir of the Psalms or any other book of sacred writing and to watch how the self-discovery unfolds. If the professional Bible controversialists would read scripture more and defend (or debunk) it less, the world would be a more serene place.

The book of Psalms is a record of the odyssey of faith, a romance without end. The Psalms have a way of commenting on our own circumstances, like an everyday narrative of the yearning world. They wait there at the historic heart of the story of God, ready to release new energies of spirit in every time of turbulence and the peace thereafter.

ABOUT THE AUTHOR

RAY WADDLE, a nationally known religion writer for two decades, was religion editor at *The Tennessean* from 1984–2001. His work has taken him across the nation, through Europe and Israel. Born in Shreveport, Louisiana, he has a journalism degree from the University of Oklahoma and a master's degree in religious studies from Vanderbilt University. He has published poetry, led retreats, and won awards for reporting. He writes widely on the subject of faith and society.

Mike DuBose